FREE TO THRIVE
STUDY GUIDE

A BIBLICAL GUIDE TO UNDERSTANDING HOW YOUR
HURT, STRUGGLES, AND DEEPEST LONGINGS
CAN LEAD TO A FULFILLING LIFE

JOSH MCDOWELL AND BEN BENNETT
WITH JOSH BLUNT

THOMAS NELSON
Since 1798

THOMAS NELSON

Free to Thrive Study Guide
© 2023 Josh McDowell Ministry

Published in Nashville, Tennessee, by Thomas Nelson. Thomas Nelson is a registered trademark of HarperCollins Christian Publishing, Inc.

Thomas Nelson titles may be purchased in bulk for educational, business, fundraising, or sales promotional use. For information, please e-mail SpecialMarkets@ThomasNelson.com.

ISBN 978-0-310-14002-3 (softcover)

ISBN 978-0-310-14019-1 (ebook)

Cover design: Micah Kandros Design
Interior design: Kait Lamphere

Printed in the United States of America

23 24 25 26 27 28 29 30 31 32 33 34 35 /TRM/ 17 16 15 14 13 12 11 10 9 8 7 6 5 4 3 2 1

To the hurting, lonely, and struggling. To the doubting, questioning, and confused. To those searching for wholeness, your purpose, and greater flourishing. May you experience healing, wholeness, and a thriving life—and know and be known by the One who makes it all possible.

CONTENTS

How to Use This Guide ix

Introduction. xi

Session One: Legitimate Longings 1

Session Two: Your Seven Longings 13

Session Three: Your Unmet Longings 23

Session Four: Identifying the Unwanted 39

Session Five: Listen to Your Longings 51

Session Six: What Your Brain Needs You to Know 61

Session Seven: You've Got the Wrong God 73

Session Eight: Seeing Yourself as God Sees You 83

Session Nine: You're Made for More 95

Session Ten: What's True for Me Is True for You 109

Session Eleven: Your Move 119

Closing Thoughts 129

Leading This Group 131

Tools for Growth

The Met and Unmet Longings Table 135

Renewing the Mind 138

Proactive Support 140

Additional Resources 141

HOW TO USE THIS GUIDE

The *Free to Thrive Study Guide* is designed to be experienced in a group setting such as a Bible study, church staff training, Sunday school class, or any small group gathering. Each session begins with a welcome section and introductory questions to get you all thinking together about the topic. You will then watch a video teaching and engage in small group discussion and sharing, including several readings from the Bible. You will close each session with a key Scripture and a time of reflection and prayer as a group.

Each person in the group should have a copy of this study guide and a Christian Bible. Whatever translation you have is fine. You are also encouraged to have a copy of the *Free to Thrive* book because reading it alongside this study guide will provide you with deeper insights and make the journey more meaningful.

To get the most out of your group experience, keep the following points in mind: First, the real growth in this study will happen as you process and apply the concepts throughout each week. Second, growth will also happen during your small group time. This is where you will discuss the content of the teaching for the week, ask questions, support one another, and learn from others as you hear what God is doing in their lives. This is true of any small group study, but the materials covered in this particular one require even more sincere, safe, and honest participation than usual. For this reason, it is important for you to be fully committed to the group and attend each session so you can build trust and rapport with other members. If you choose merely to go through the motions, or if you refrain from participating, there is little chance you will find what you're looking for during this study, and you will be detracting from the experience of others who can benefit from your contributions and encouragement.

Third, remember that the goal of your small group is to serve as a place where people can share, learn about God, and build intimacy and friendship. For this reason, please make every effort for your group to remain a safe place. This means being honest about your thoughts and feelings and listening carefully to everyone else's opinion. It also means keeping everything your group shares confidential. Doing so will foster a rewarding sense of community in your group and create a place where people can heal, be challenged, and grow spiritually. Resist the temptation to view your fellow group members as problems to fix; everyone will learn more and grow faster when treated with dignity and respect. If you are tempted to try and solve a problem someone might be having or to correct his or her thinking, theology, or contributions without being asked, please refrain—this is not the purpose of your small group time.

Following your group time, reflect on the material you've covered by engaging in the *Deeper Dive* learning activities after each session. These are provided for you to use between meetings of your group to dig deeper into the material. Note that even if you are unable to finish your between-sessions personal study, you should still attend the group study session. You are still wanted and welcome at the group.

In addition to all these materials, you will notice that throughout the video series you'll hear stories of people who have also faced hurt and struggles but still found real healing and thriving lives. Keep in mind that the videos, real examples, discussion questions, and activities are simply meant to kick-start your thoughts. Ultimately, the goal of all these things is that you will be open to hear what God is saying and apply it to your life. As you go through this study, be listening and be open to God as he begins to heal you and set you free to thrive!

↗ **Note:** If you are a group leader, additional resources are provided at the back of this guide to help you lead your group members through the study.

INTRODUCTION

Something isn't right. You may not be able to put your finger on it yet, but deep inside you know that somehow your life isn't as free and full as it could be. Maybe you're joining this study because you know you've been stuck in unhealthy behaviors, thoughts, or relationship patterns. Perhaps you're experiencing unresolved hurts, shame, or struggles with your view of God. The pain and confusion that these struggles bring can be crippling. We want you to know that there is hope and there are real answers that can bring lasting freedom. Or, maybe you're engaging this material because you have a sense that God has more for you and you want to experience a thriving life—one of spiritual, emotional, and relational health and wholeness. You too will find real answers in these materials.

Full disclosure—this study, and the steps to healing it offers, will not be entirely easy or painless. Real growth requires real risk. One of the most essential parts of emotional and spiritual healing is self-disclosure in safe relationships; this may feel daunting, but the process is meant to be a team effort—God designed you for relationship with himself and with others. If you can accept the risk of entrusting yourself to others and allowing them, guided by the Holy Spirit, to journey with you and be used by God to comfort and challenge you, you will find the joy, satisfaction, and abundant life you have been longing for.

It's high time we face the underlying factors driving our unwanted behaviors and struggles and begin a journey to healing through biblical, well-researched, and time-tested principles. You are not made to flounder and flail; you are made for more. You are made to thrive. Jesus offers you healing, health, wholeness, and true satisfaction. Through timeless biblical principles, backed by research, you'll find solutions in this study that God will use to set you free. We invite you into your journey of healing from hurts and overcoming your unwanted behaviors by engaging your unmet longings. Your thriving life awaits . . .

SESSION ONE

LEGITIMATE LONGINGS

WELCOME

In Psalm 23, King David of Israel says, "The Lord is my shepherd; I lack nothing." Some have said that we cease to have desires when we are living in proper communion with God. Nothing could be further from the truth—you may be surprised to hear that desire is a good gift from God, intended to lead us to healing and peace. God doesn't ease our longings by removing them; he completes them by satisfying us fully through himself and other people. In fact, the Bible assures us that being around God even *heightens* our desires and leads us to an ever-increasing enjoyment of his presence and love.

So, what is going wrong with our desires and longings? How are we falling short of the abundant life Jesus promised us? Many of us look at the seemingly picture-perfect lives portrayed by others and assume we are the only ones missing the party. We try our best to suppress our disappointment and conceal the compulsions, addictions, and anxious fidgets we have adopted behind the scenes as ways of feeling a little better for a moment or two. In the end we feel even more alone and isolated, believing that if anyone knew what we struggle with, we would be rejected and abandoned. Maybe you think about this a lot, or perhaps you have gotten really good at thinking about anything *but* this.

If you can admit to yourself that any of this sounds familiar, and if you are willing to start being honest about it, this session will get you started on the path of understanding your God-given longings and what might be going wrong in your pursuit of them. This path isn't for the faint of heart, but it *is* for those who are ready to admit they want more: Jesus himself assures us that "Blessed are those who hunger and thirst for righteousness, for they will be filled" (Matthew 5:6).

SHARE

BEFORE SHARING: This study will touch on many tender spots in each of our hearts. If he or she hasn't done so yet, be sure that your leader takes a moment now to go over the basics of confidentiality, respect, and caring that will govern this group's interactions. (See the How to Use This Guide *section for more.) Take a moment to pray together and ask for safety and respect to characterize all of your time together.*

- What led you to join this study? Are there any particular outcomes you are hoping to experience by the study's end?
- On a scale from 1–10, how intensely are you currently experiencing a sense of longing for something more in your life, relationships, and faith?

WATCH

Play the video for *Session 1: Legitimate Longings* from the *Free to Thrive Video Study*. As you watch, use the following outline to record any thoughts, questions, or key points that stand out to you.

The Heart behind This Series
- Josh's personal testimony

_____

_____

_____

A Cocktail of Compulsions

- Statistics and examples of unwanted behaviors

_____

_____

_____

_____

God-Given Longings

- God has a good plan for our longings.

_____

_____

_____

_____

The Fruit of Unmet Longings

_____

_____

_____

_____

A Thriving Life

- Ben's personal testimony

_____

_____

_____

_____

_____

- Throughout this series you'll hear stories of people who have also faced hurt and struggles but still found real healing and thriving lives. Meet our brave friends who you'll be hearing more from:
    - Audrey Hardin

_____

○ Ernie and Jackie Chambers

_____

○ Monica Bailey

_____

○ Fedel (Anthony Flagg)

_____

DISCUSS

With your group, discuss what you have just watched and explore these concepts in Scripture. Use the following questions to guide your discussion.

1 Some other world religions tell their adherents that desire is bad because it leads us to distress and disappointment. How do you feel about the possibility that God actually designed us with longings as a good part of his plan for us? If this concept feels strange to you, why do you think that is? What teachings, experiences, or troubles have led you to mistrust your longings?

_____

_____

_____

_____

2 In the next lesson we will actually name the seven key longings God has written in our hearts. For this session, let's start the discussion by taking a guess: what do you imagine two or three of your God-given longings might be?

_____

_____

_____

_____

3 As you think of Josh's and Ben's stories, or of the others shown in this video, how common do you think such experiences of hurt and disappointment are in the world? By comparison, how often have you heard those things discussed in churches or Christian friendships? Why do you think that is? In what ways do you hope to improve on this through your own effort and honesty in this group?

_____

_____

_____

_____

_____

4 **Read:** Ecclesiastes 3:9–13. What are these verses saying about God's design for desires? What does God expect will happen to us when we have eternity written in our hearts but are not able to fully sort it out (v. 11)? If God wants us to have joy in all our work on earth but has also created us with an unfathomable desire for eternity, what are we supposed to do?

_____

_____

_____

_____

_____

5 **Read:** Psalm 63. What are some of the longings the psalmist (King David of Israel) says he is experiencing? Can you relate to any of them? How does he say God has met him in those desires? Have you ever met someone in person who was as hungry for God as this? If not, what do you imagine it would look like today?

_____

_____

_____

_____

_____

6 Psalm 63 describes God being able to fill our hearts like the richest and most satisfying foods. What would that food be for you? Can you think of a time when walking with Jesus made you feel that full and delighted? (It's good to be honest—if the answer is "no" today, that just means God is preparing some amazing experiences for your future.)

_____

_____

_____

_____

_____

_____

7 In his lecture "The Weight of Glory," Christian writer C. S. Lewis said that, when it comes to longings, our problem is not desiring too much, but rather too little! He insists that our longings are not too strong, but actually too weak and misdirected. What are some of the ways you see people growing weaker, more hardened, and less sensitive in their longings?

_____

_____

_____

_____

_____

Read and Reflect

In each session, you will be given a key verse (or verses) to learn from one of the passages covered in the video teaching. This week your suggested verses are Isaiah 55:1–2:

> Come, all you who are thirsty,
>
> come to the waters;

and you who have no money,

come, buy and eat!

Come, buy wine and milk

without money and without cost.

Why spend money on what is not bread,

and your labor on what does not satisfy?

Listen, listen to me, and eat what is good,

and you will delight in the richest of fare.

—Isaiah 55:1–2

Read this passage three or four times, either silently as individuals or out loud as a group. What is its message? Consider committing part or all of this passage to memory over the next week.

Respond

In this session, Josh and Ben have led us to consider the legitimate role our longings play in our faith journey. What is one big lesson that jumps out in your heart as a matter for prayer and reflection so far, and/or what is one specific action you can commit to try between this session and the next?

Pray

Close your group time by praying in any of the following directions:

- Ask the Holy Spirit to purify your desires and help you get in touch with your God-given longings. If you have been too easily satisfied with lesser things, invite God to increase the intensity of your hunger for him.
- Pray that your group will be an honest and safe place where people can come out of hiding, share their burdens, and fully engage the study as a healthy team.
- Thank God for loving you enough to plant deep longings in your heart to lead you to himself; thank him, also, for loving you too much to let anything but him fully satisfy those longings.

- Thank God for the testimonies you saw in the video, then ask him to produce equally honest and authentic testimonies out of your group's work together.
- Invite Jesus to begin disrupting and exposing any counterfeit or substitute pathways you might be following in vain attempts to satisfy your God-given longings. This is a dangerous prayer, but a powerful one!

DEEPER DIVE

SESSION ONE:
Legitimate Longings

Go deeper into the material you have covered in this session by engaging in the following between-session learning experiences. After each study section, you will find some practical exercises to help you engage with the material more personally before the group meets again. You may feel led to share some of what you learn with your group—although some things may stay less specific and more private. Either way, these opportunities are part of the process and we encourage you to try them.

A VISION FOR WHOLENESS

Read . . .

We don't become a new person by changing our behavior; we discover the person we already are in Christ and behave accordingly. Many of us have been urged to start doing things in order to activate the process of spiritual growth. Well-meaning Christians challenge new believers to study the Bible, memorize verses, attend church as often as possible, share their faith with others, and replace old sinful habits with patterns of godly living. Sometimes in our good intentions of wanting to see people rooted in their faith, we convey that their spiritual activity will transform their spiritual identity.

We are all for these spiritual practices, but studious involvement in these does not transform us. Studying the Bible, going to church, and sharing our faith doesn't cause God to declare us loved or valued. He already has declared us loved and valued because that is who we really are in Christ. We don't *do* our way into our identity as God's beloved children; we *are* God's beloved children. When we realize that we are "God's masterpiece" and learn to occupy that reality, we can live accordingly and "do the good things he planned for us long ago," as Ephesians 2:10 (NLT) says.

God designed us to live a thriving life of wholeness spiritually (being made right with God and enjoying a personal, intimate relationship with him), emotionally (seeing ourselves as God sees us and being in tune with our inner world), and relationally (having relationships of being fully known and fully loved and sharing Christ's love with others). When we are living *from* wholeness and *into* wholeness in all these areas, we begin to experience maximum satisfaction in life. We live according to our design as humans and experience what we were created to experience.

Reflect . . .

- Ask God to give you a vision for wholeness; invite the Holy Spirit to inspire your imagination and show you a picture of who you would be if you were living from a place of being healed and complete. Write down what you pictured . . .

_____

_____

_____

_____

- Have you tried spiritual practices as a means of *doing* your way into wholeness? Which ones? List them below. How has this worked for you so far?

_____

_____

_____

_____

Assess . . .

1 What are a few unwanted behaviors that are holding you back?

_____

_____

_____

2 What emotions do you feel about these unwanted behaviors?

_____

_____

_____

3 How do you really feel God views you as a result of these behaviors?

_____

_____

_____

4 Do you really believe Jesus blesses the longings behind your unwanted behaviors and wants to satisfy those in healthy ways?

_____

_____

_____

SESSION TWO

YOUR SEVEN LONGINGS

WELCOME

When you think of all the many things you want in this life, the idea that there are *only* seven key longings in the depths of our hearts may seem surprising. We all know how very skilled we can be in wanting more. But the universality of these seven is demonstrably true. All of our other expressions of desire and our pursuit of satisfaction ultimately stem back to one of these seven key God-given longings. Just imagine how much it would be worth if we could understand these seven drives, map out how they influence our choices, behaviors, and values, and then see them all increasingly satisfied by Jesus in healthy, sustainable ways. Well, you won't have to imagine for too long; this study intends to lead you into that exact path.

Others may be daunted by the prospect of exploring all that need. Perhaps you have generally adopted a negative view of desire and aren't yet comfortable exploring your longings, fearing that this will lead to more frustration. The reality is that Jesus promised that we could "have life and have it abundantly" (John 10:10 ESV), and this is an assurance that he has a good plan to give us a full and satisfying life. We can enter into this life right now, even before we get to heaven, if we start understanding the way God is using our longings to lead us to him and how perfect his plan is to meet those longings through relationships with him and with others.

SHARE

BEFORE SHARING: Take a moment now to review the basics of confidentiality, respect, and caring that will govern this group's interactions. (See the How to Use This Guide *section for more.)*

- How has God been keeping last session's contents on your mind since the group last met? Have you had any new thoughts, discoveries, confirmations, or questions since then?
- Have you seen God answer any of the prayers we prayed together during the last session in the time between meetings?
- What are some unique longings you suspect won't be on the list of seven, but which nevertheless seem pretty important to you? (Keep them in mind during this study—you may be surprised to see that some of your answers actually show up as variations on one of the seven. If that happens, be sure to point it out to the group.)

WATCH

Play the video for *Session 2: Your Seven Longings* from the *Free to Thrive Video Study*. As you watch, use the following outline to record any thoughts, questions, or key points that stand out to you.

- Monica's experience

_____

_____

_____

_____

Beyond Maslow

- Maslow's surprisingly biblical hierarchy of needs

_____

_____

_____

What Everyone Wants—The Seven Longings

1 **Appreciation:** to be _____ or _____ for what you have done.

2 **Affection:** to be cared for with _____ touch or _____ engagement.

3 **Access:** to have the _____ emotional and physical _____ of key figures.

4 **Attention:** to be known and _____ with someone _____ your world.

5 **Affirmation of Feelings:** to have our feelings affirmed, _____, or _____ by others.

Two Especially Unmet Longings of Today

6 **Acceptance:** to be _____, loved, and _____ of as you are, no matter what.

    Ice Cream for the Losers

- Josh shares a poignant example of Acceptance—no matter what.

_____

_____

_____

- Fedel's experience (Anthony Flagg)

_____

_____

_____

7 **Assurance of Safety:** to feel safe, _____, and provided for emotionally, physically, and _____.

The Example Set by the Early Christians

- Acts 2:44–47 shows the early church meeting the need for Assurance of Safety through loving community.

_____

_____

_____

DISCUSS

With your group, discuss what you have just watched and explore these concepts in Scripture. Use the following questions to guide your discussion.

1 Many people are very out of touch with their hearts, longings, and unmet needs. In fact, some have made an art out of hiding or ignoring such feelings. On a scale from 1–10, how aware would you say you are about your own longings and how well-met they currently are? How can your group help you process that?

_____

_____

_____

_____

2 **Read:** Romans 8:26–27. How does this passage affect you? If the Holy Spirit knows what we need and how to pray for us *even when we don't*, how might he be using this study to help us along right now? Is it possible he has led us all here as another way of making connections between our hearts and God's?

_____

_____

_____

_____

3 Josh shared a story about a time he used ice cream to teach about Acceptance. Can you think of an example in your own life when someone made you feel deeply accepted? What gesture, words, or actions did this person use to get through to you? Have you ever copied that move with others?

_____

_____

_____

_____

_____

4 In the video, a study from Harvard University was quoted which indicated that good relationships decisively contribute to our happiness and health. Can you name one or two good relationships God is using right now to make you more joyful and healthy? How could you reach out and thank these people this week?

_____

_____

_____

_____

_____

5 **Read:** Romans 5:6–8. Why was it just the right time for Christ to die for us when we were weak and stuck in our sin? Does this tell you anything about God's method of extending acceptance? If we were to show acceptance using the same pattern, who is someone who needs your acceptance and when would be the right time to show this person?

_____

_____

_____

_____

_____

6 Do you think there is a difference between acceptance of a person and approval of his/her actions and choices? Go back to Romans 5:6–8 as a reference point and see how God handled that challenge with us. How could we follow his example in the messy situations that sometimes pop up when we are seeking to truly offer acceptance to people who aren't yet ready to follow God? What did this cost Jesus, and what might it cost us?

_____

_____

_____

_____

_____

_____

7 **Read:** Matthew 6:25–34. What does Jesus say about God's provision for us? In thinking about the need for Assurance of Safety, what assurances does he give us (in this passage or elsewhere)?

_____

_____

_____

_____

_____

Read and Reflect

In each session, you will be given a key verse (or verses) to learn from one of the passages covered in the video teaching. This week your suggested verse is Psalm 84:10:

> Better is one day in your courts
>> than a thousand elsewhere;

> I would rather be a doorkeeper in the house of my God
>
> than dwell in the tents of the wicked.
>
> —Psalm 84:10

Read this passage three or four times, either silently as individuals or out loud as a group. What is its message about longing and satisfaction? Consider committing part or all of this passage to memory over the next week.

Respond

This session lets you know what your seven God-given longings are and explains a little bit about how they are meant to function in concert to experience the abundant life Jesus promised. What is one big lesson that jumps out in your heart as a matter for prayer and reflection so far, and/or what is one specific action you can commit to try between this session and the next?

Pray

Close your group time by praying in any of the following directions:

- Thank God as a group for the longings he has hardwired into you all. Thank him for using this group, even now, as a way to satisfy some of these longings.
- Pray specifically for anyone in your group who admits to feeling a little exposed and vulnerable as we look into this material—each lesson can hit close to home for some people more than others. Take time to rejoice with those who rejoice and mourn with those who mourn.
- As you think about the world right now, some groups or individuals may stand out as especially neglected in the meeting of their needs and longings. Take time as a group to pray for these people, and ask God to show you if there is any other way you could help them as a team.
- Next time, the group will discuss the unmet longings in each of our hearts and what this condition does to us. Pray that everyone in the group is able to come rested, honest, and ready to offer safety, authenticity, and kindness to one another.

Answers for Blanks Above . . .

Here are the words that complete the blanks in the Seven Longings descriptions above:

1. thanked, encouraged
2. gentle, emotional
3. consistent, presence
4. understood, entering
5. validated, confirmed
6. included, approved
7. protected, financially

SESSION TWO:
Your Seven Longings

THE WHOLENESS APOLOGETIC

Read...

When we experience our Seven Longings being met in healthy ways with God and others, we experience "true wholeness." This forms the basis of what we call the Wholeness Apologetic model pictured on the next page. Throughout this study we will explore each aspect of the model, occasionally referring back to the diagram. We'll explain why we struggle to experience this life of true wholeness we were intended to live and how we can reclaim that divine design.

Assess...

1 What longings were met in healthy ways before your teenage years?

_____

_____

_____

_____

_____

_____

THE WHOLENESS APOLOGETIC

Supporting God's design for human flourishing in all areas of life.
We experience this primarily through the fulfillment of our
Seven Longings with God, self, and others.

TRUE WHOLENESS

SPIRITUAL BROKENNESS
Cuts us off from true wholeness and connection with God due to the fall in Genesis 3.

FURTHER WHOLENESS
In a combined effort with the Holy Spirit (Rom 8:13; Phil 2:13), we take steps to grow and experience healing.

FURTHER BROKENNESS
From unmet longings, others' choices, and ours.

GOD'S DESIGN FOR HEALING
Asking Jesus for healing – Ps 147:3
Identifying unmet longings – Prov 4:23
Experiencing met longings by God and others – Ps 145:16, 19; Eccles 4:9–10; James 5:16; 1 Thess 5:11; John 13:34
Replacing lies with truth, and unwanted behaviors with thriving behaviors – Rom 12:2
Forgiveness – 2 Cor 2:5–11
Understand your cycle in Eph 4:17–19

UNMET LONGINGS LEAD TO UNWANTED BEHAVIORS
We react to our hurt and unmet longings and get stuck.
1 Pet 3:9; Rom 12:17; Gen 50:15–17; 1 Sam 21–24; John 4; Job 3; Jer 10:19; Ps 38:5; Eph 4:17–19

CHOOSING WHOLENESS
Spiritually, Emotionally, Relationally

2 Who were the people who met your longings in healthy ways?

_____

_____

_____

3 What longing are you most thankful was met growing up?

_____

_____

_____

4 If you could have one longing met today, what would it be and why?

_____

_____

_____

SESSION THREE

YOUR UNMET LONGINGS

WELCOME

There are some things in this life that we first experience as an absence. For example, we often only start looking for justice once we have become familiar with its absence—injustice. Or, we first start caring about dignity after feeling the sting of its absence—indignity. Unfortunately, some of our longings came to us first (and/or most consistently) as an absence. Some of us became aware how important Assurance of Safety is through its absence—abuse. Some of us realized that we needed Affection only when it was withheld in our homes or our marriages and we instead experienced coldness. Some started hungering for Acceptance after a string of rejections.

This session deals with a painful and profound experience everyone goes through in this world: Unmet Longings. This experience is bound to happen, especially when we are infused with these seven deep and persistent longings and yet live in a world so affected by sin. The world and its inhabitants—at least in their current state—can't help but leave us with hurts and wounds that interfere with healthy satisfaction of our longings. Thankfully, Jesus generously offers himself and his body, the church, as resources in healing these injuries. But the first step is to identify and confess the attacks and absences that have affected us up to this point.

SHARE

- Has God shown up in any interesting ways since last time? How did he answer the prayers we prayed together in our last session? Have you made any discoveries as you processed the contents thus far?
- As you think about the Seven Longings from the last session, which of the seven are you most eager to learn more about? Which are you dreading talking about the most? Either (or both) may be areas of unmet need—pay attention during the current session and see if this is the case.

WATCH

Play the video for *Session 3: Your Unmet Longings* from the *Free to Thrive Video Study*. As you watch, use the following outline to record any thoughts, questions, or key points that stand out to you.

Uninvited

- Ben's skateboarding story

_____

_____

_____

_____

- Fedel's experience (Anthony Flagg)

_____

_____

_____

_____

Everybody Hurts Sometimes
- David's dark chapter

_____

_____

_____

_____

Attacks and Absences
- Attacks

_____

_____

_____

- Absences

_____

_____

_____

- Differences in intensity and duration

_____

_____

_____

- Audrey's experience

_____

_____

_____

- Differences in each individual

_____

_____

_____

When Longings Go Unmet

- Sharon's story

  _____

  _____

  _____

  _____

- Ivan's story

  _____

  _____

  _____

  _____

- Monica's experience

  _____

  _____

  _____

  _____

The Pain and the Thirst

- Unmet longings create deep pain and insatiable thirst that drive us to find satisfaction.

  _____

  _____

  _____

- Longings that remain unmet reinforce and deepen the hurts and lies that caused them.

  _____

  _____

  _____

Read Your Own Life

- We need God and one another to break the cycle of pain and new hurts.

  _____

  _____

  _____

- We must prayerfully process our stories—including the attacks, absences, and hurts—with safe, trustworthy people.

  _____

  _____

  _____

- We are assured that God cares and has already provided everything needed to meet us in this process. He has given his only Son to bear our hurts—why would he hold out on us now?

  _____

  _____

  _____

DISCUSS

With your group, discuss what you have just watched and explore these concepts in Scripture. Use the following questions to guide your discussion.

↗ **A note about sharing deep hurts:** Most people do not feel safe disclosing every wound in every setting. If you think you would prefer to share something in an alternate, appropriate configuration besides the whole group (separated by gender, a triad, with a mentor, etc.), please tell your leader. Also, if your spouse is attending with you and either of you is a source of unmet longings for the other, please consult together about ways to share honestly but respectfully so as to avoid dishonoring each other in front of the group.

1 How do you feel about taking time to continue looking back and unpacking your past experiences and hurts? Which one of these statements most matches your mood: (a) I'm eager to dive in—I know there's some stuff there that needs airing out; (b) I'm terrified to poke the hornets' nest—I say let sleeping dogs lie; (c) I don't really think there's much to talk about—I haven't experienced much hurt; (d) I think this is a bad idea—it sounds like psychobabble, dishonoring parents, and self-indulgent whining; or (e) I honestly feel a little numb and stuck—I'm not sure why, but there are big parts of my past I can't really remember that well.

_____

_____

_____

_____

2 What were some of the absences and attacks that may have contributed to your unmet longings, pain, and thirst? Are these situations in the past, or are some of them current? How are new hurts compounding the pain or adding to the loss?

_____

_____

_____

_____

3 **Read:** Proverbs 17:17. Many are afraid to share their hurts and unmet longings with others. Why do you think this is? How does this proverb assure us about the heart of a biblical, true friend? Name some friends you have who are like this. If your list is short, can the members of this group help?

_____

_____

_____

_____

_____

4 It takes some time to sort things out—you may be aware of an attack or absence but can't yet identify any present unmet longings, even though you suspect they exist. Similarly, you may have a profound longing that isn't easily connected to a particular event. If either of these situations is the case, share with the members of the group and let them help you play detective over the sessions ahead.

_____

_____

_____

_____

_____

5 **Read:** Isaiah 53:4–6. What do these verses personally mean to you as you begin the process of reflecting on your past hurts via attack, absence, and other types of brokenness? What does this passage tell you about the role Jesus wants to play (and has already played) in your process of healing?

_____

_____

_____

_____

_____

6 As you dive into some of your past experiences, you may find yourself hurt, angry, ashamed, or frightened all over again. This is understandable; however, you may also be pleasantly surprised to see how good it feels to tell someone and not be judged. Why do you think this is so? How can this group support and encourage you in this process?

_____

_____

_____

_____

_____

Read and Reflect

> The LORD is close to the brokenhearted
>
> and saves those who are crushed in spirit.
>
> The righteous person may have many troubles,
>
> but the LORD delivers him from them all.
>
> —Psalm 34:18–19

Read this passage three or four times, either silently as individuals or out loud as a group. What is its message? Consider committing part or all of this passage to memory over the next week.

Respond

This session has begun your journey of unearthing and naming past hurts and the unmet longings they triggered. What is one big lesson that jumps out in your heart as a matter for prayer and reflection so far, and/or what is one specific action you can commit to try between this session and the next?

Pray

Close your group time by praying in any of the following directions:

- Many things may have begun to be unearthed in this discussion; take time to pray specifically for anything shared in the discussion or for anyone having a particularly hard (or even overwhelmingly positive) time.
- Pray for all those over whom you have influence and opportunity to appropriately meet God-given longings (especially any kids, siblings, coworkers, spouse, or good friends). Ask that God will help you to care for them well and avoid the kinds of hurts you are hearing about in this group.
- Thank God for how he is at work in and through your unmet longings. He has a plan to use them for good (Romans 8:28).

- Pray that God will bring at least one instance of new satisfaction and joy in one of your areas of pain or thirst. Leave the details up to him and invite him to surprise you—just ask for the good gift of some refreshment, encouragement, and forward progress.
- Pray for spiritual protection over one another. Sometimes digging into these topics stirs up spiritual resistance, so ask for God's protection and strength over each person in your group.

SESSION THREE:
Your Unmet Longings

A VISION FOR WHOLENESS

Read . . .

Psychologist Arielle Schwartz writes:

Childhood traumas can range from having faced extreme violence and neglect to having confronted feelings of not belonging, being unwanted, or being chronically misunderstood. You may have grown up in an environment where your curiosity and enthusiasm were constantly devalued. Perhaps you were brought up in a family where your parents had unresolved traumas of their own, which impaired their ability to attend to your emotional needs. Or, you may have faced vicious sexual or physical attacks. In all such situations, you learn to compensate by developing defenses around your most vulnerable parts.[*]

Numerous factors influence how deeply and how long these unmet longings hurt us. We can categorize their sources in two ways. Some come from *attacks*; they include name-calling and other insults, manipulation, teasing, sexual or physical abuse,

---

[*] Arielle Schwartz, *The Complex PTSD Workbook* (Berkeley, CA: Althea Press, 2016), 11.

and more. Other hurts we feel come from *absences*, such as a parent who leaves—or one who is distant emotionally or physically—as well as from a lack of affirming or loving words, being ignored by friends or family members, being dismissed as unimportant, etc.

Both attacks and absences can hurt deeply. Attacks and absences always leave us with unmet longings, whether fleeting or lasting. A single attack of high intensity, such as being sexually or physically abused, can cause a lifetime of pain. However, so can attacks that are less intense, such as being ridiculed and called names on a childhood playground or being singled out and ostracized for your race or gender. These can also inflict a lifetime of hurt upon our souls.

Similarly, the pain of unmet longings may follow onetime absences of high intensity, such as a parent missing our biggest football game of the year, being stood up by a date, or a parent deserting the family. But enduring or recurring absences, such as a parent being emotionally unengaged, being excluded from important office meetings, or hardly ever feeling affirmed or approved of by significant people in our lives can also leave a deep and lasting wound.

As uniquely created individuals, of course, we all respond to attacks and absences differently. Something that devastates one individual may have little effect on another.

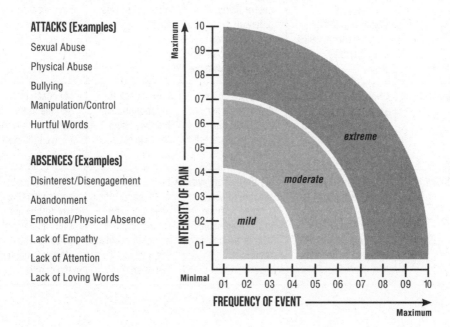

ATTACKS (Examples)
Sexual Abuse
Physical Abuse
Bullying
Manipulation/Control
Hurtful Words

ABSENCES (Examples)
Disinterest/Disengagement
Abandonment
Emotional/Physical Absence
Lack of Empathy
Lack of Attention
Lack of Loving Words

I've heard many people say, "I've had a relatively easy life compared to others," but one person's pain never truly compares with another. And ignoring, dismissing, or downplaying the effects of attacks and absences on our own lives may prevent us from dealing with our hurts, healing from them, and moving forward into the best possible future. The diagram on the previous page depicts how both attacks and absences can lead to varying levels of pain in our souls. You'll see that both the frequency of a specific type of painful event and the intensity of that painful event directly correlate to the level of pain felt—whether mild, moderate, or extreme.

When Longings Go Unmet

Just as we respond to attacks and absences differently, so it helps to understand how different unmet longings can look and feel in our lives. Unmet longings may vary, not only according to their intensity and frequency, but also according to their source, as the examples in the following table illustrate.

UNMET LONGINGS TABLE

Longings	Mom / Dad	Siblings / Relatives	Friends	Others
1. Acceptance	• Dad never said, "I love you" • Mom regularly treated me as weird or different	• My brother teased me for being different • Grandpa never seemed to want to spend time with me	• My best friends often said I was weird	• Teachers valued me based on my grades
2. Appreciation	• Never heard Mom say "I'm proud of you," or "Great job"	• Often helped my sister clean her room but was never thanked; felt used	• I often cook for my roommates, but they never help me clean up	• My coach often told me to try harder even when I played my best
3. Affection	• Dad didn't give me hugs or comfort me when I was upset • Mom often didn't pick me up when I wanted to be held	• My brother always seemed to be irritated with me rather than being kind in words and actions	• My best friend is often stand-offish physically and refrains from anything deemed "sappy" or "emotional"	• I told my husband about my difficult day and he just said "that sucks" when I wanted physical affection and comfort

Longings	Mom / Dad	Siblings / Relatives	Friends	Others
4. Access	• Dad was often gone on work trips or at the office • Mom was emotionally distant	• My sister avoided me growing up	• I've spent many Friday nights alone recently without friends	• My boss is seldom there when I need his help
5. Attention	• Dad never cared too much about my hobbies or interests • Mom never entered my world; said my interests were "silly"	• My grandma never asked me how my games were going or what I enjoyed about sports	• My best friends only want to hang out if we do what they want to do	• My life coach talks about himself all the time rather than seeking to understand me
6. Affirmation of Feelings	• It was unacceptable to be sad or upset in my family growing up • Mom often told me not to be so whiny	• I recently told my sister how hard my year was and she told me I was partly to blame	• Growing up, my friends often said I was overreacting	• I told my teacher how sad I was about my struggles with math and he said I just wasn't a math person
7. Assurance of Safety	• My parents lived paycheck-to-paycheck so I grew up worrying about money and my basic needs	• I was picked on and beat up as a kid and my brother never stood up for me	• My best friends teased me quite a bit	• I was sexually abused by a family friend

Assess...

1 Of the Seven Longings we've discussed in this study, which would you say are the two you find yourself thinking about or desiring most?

_____

_____

_____

2 In what ways have these two longings gone unmet in the past year? Throughout life growing up?

_____

_____

_____

3 Can you identify moments when these longings went unmet through attacks? Absences?

_____

_____

_____

4 Try praying this prayer of David before you complete the "Depth of Longings Assessment":

Search me, God, and know my heart;
    test me and know my anxious thoughts.
See if there is any offensive way in me,
    and lead me in the way everlasting. (Psalm 139:23–24)

↗ DEPTH OF LONGINGS ASSESSMENT ↗

This assessment, developed in collaboration with Dr. Ted Roberts, is intended to help you identify and understand the unmet longings that have been holding you back in your journey toward wholeness. Please check each item with a Y (for "Yes") or N (for "No").

Y N

___ ___ I have trouble stopping certain actions even though they are unhelpful/destructive

___ ___ I repeat destructive behaviors over and over, which started early in my life

___ ___ I often have increased sexual desires when I am lonely

___ ___ I feel loyal to people even though they have hurt me

___ ___ I use the internet, streaming media, eating, and hobbies as a way to check out

___ ___ I repeatedly put off certain tasks

___ ___ I feel badly about myself because of shameful experiences in my past

___ ___ I hide some of my behaviors from others

___ ___ After engaging in an unwanted behavior, I feel sad afterward

___ ___ I feel controlled at times by my unwanted behaviors

___ ___ I fear the rejection of other people

___ ___ I think what I do is never good enough

___ ___ I feel I'm not worthy of love

___ ___ I fear that I am a bother to people

___ ___ I feel unknown and misunderstood

___ ___ I believe that my thoughts and opinions don't matter

___ ___ I have fears about my safety, finances, or emotional needs

Scoring

Count how many statements to which you answered "Yes."

Total "Yes" Responses ___

A score of 6 or more "Yes" responses indicates significant longings may have gone unmet in both the past and present. We recommend finding a professional therapist to help you navigate these unresolved areas of unmet longings and pain. This assessment is not conclusive, but rather meant to be an indication of the depths of unmet longings and hurt in your life.

IDENTIFYING THE UNWANTED

WELCOME

We all have them—those behaviors that come out of hiding when we aren't at our best. Sometimes others around us are very aware of them and point them out as undesirable. Other times we try to keep them so secret that only God would know. Some of these behaviors are clearly sins, while others like anxiety or depression are not. Still other behaviors are actually good things being used for an unhealthy reason. No created thing, experience, person, or pleasure can substitute for God, and when we try to use these as stand-ins, they turn from gifts into traps. If you have ever found some temporary relief or satisfaction in a behavior, only to find yourself needing more and more, yet feeling less and less, you have experienced an unwanted behavior.

This session will help you understand what these unwanted behaviors look like, where they might have started, and how they constitute a poor coping mechanism in light of your longings and needs. As we dive in, you may feel called out—we're often pretty attached to our false comforts, and nobody likes having these pointed out as out-of-control behavior. As you watch the video and discuss as a group, plan on adopting both humility (when your weak spots are on display) and gentleness (when it's someone else's turn in the hot seat). Regardless of how we feel in the short term, this lesson is a major blow to the chains that hold us back from thriving.

SHARE

- During the last session, you prayed that God would bring at least one instance of new satisfaction and joy in one of your areas of pain or thirst. Did you remember to watch for an answer? How did God answer that prayer?
- What are one or two things that can lift up your spirits on a bad day? Have you ever found yourself going too far in using them to feel better?
- Have you ever seen an excessive coping mechanism at work in someone you love? What was that like? What longing-gone-wrong do you think was driving this person? How did it affect you?

WATCH

Play the video for *Session 4: Identifying the Unwanted* from the *Free to Thrive Video Study*. As you watch, use the following outline to record any thoughts, questions, or key points that stand out to you.

- Fedel's experience (Anthony Flagg)

_____

_____

_____

Longing for Connection
- More of Ben's story

_____

_____

_____

Futility and Failure

- Romans 7 describes a futile cycle that occurs when we try to satisfy our longings but end up out of control and frustrated.

_____

_____

_____

_____

- Monica's experience

_____

_____

_____

_____

Unhealthy Attempts to Cope as an Individual

_____

_____

_____

_____

_____

Unhealthy Attempts to Cope in Relationships: 4 Main Stances

1 **The Pleaser Stance:** Does whatever it takes to keep others happy, to keep judgment and anger away, and to prevent other people from leaving.

_____

_____

_____

- Audrey's experience

_____

_____

_____

2 **The Blamer Stance:** Points fingers at others, pouring out anger, judgment, and shame on other people.

_____

_____

_____

3 **The Reasoner Stance:** Uses reason and intellect to try to vindicate themselves, prove another person wrong, and win the argument.

_____

_____

_____

4 **The Withdrawer Stance:** Takes an apathetic stance, convinced that the deeper stress-filled issues in life are better avoided rather than engaged.

_____

_____

_____

How the Cycle Works

- Ephesians 4:17–21 shows a clear and compelling biblical breakdown of how unwanted behaviors imprison us.

_____

_____

_____

_____

Putting Off and Putting On

- The following verses, in Ephesians 4:22–24, show us what to do about it: put off the old and put on the new.

_____

_____

_____

_____

- The first step to doing this is to identify your unwanted behaviors and when/where they began.

_____

_____

_____

_____

DISCUSS

With your group, discuss what you have just watched and explore these concepts in Scripture. Use the following questions to guide your discussion.

1 List some of the sinful things we think of first when we talk about unwanted behaviors. How common are these, in your experience? Is there an amount of such behaviors that would be acceptable in our society? What about with God? People often think they have made friends with such behaviors and will be able to stay in charge—how does that usually work out?

_____

_____

_____

_____

2 We often struggle to see the consequences that unwanted behaviors have on God, ourselves, and others. What are some of the consequences of the unwanted behaviors you identified in question 1?

_____

_____

_____

_____

_____

3 **Read:** Galatians 5:19–21. This is a biblical picture of what it looks like when we allow sin-based, unwanted behaviors to run the show. It is what would happen to all of us if sin were to have its way with us. Nobody who ends up in such extreme bondage started off in that deplorable condition. Take a minute to guess what each of the things in this passage's list looked like in its beginning stage. How does this relate to your answers to the previous question about tolerating sin?

_____

_____

_____

_____

4 Now for a harder task: List some of the really good and noble things that can turn into unwanted behaviors if we misuse them. How common is this phenomenon, in your experience? How do people usually react at first when someone is coping in such ways? Have you ever seen these behaviors go wrong for someone? Even if they don't go outwardly wrong, what effect do you think using such behavioral extremes to control our lives and soothe our hurts has on our hearts?

_____

_____

_____

_____

5 Of the four relationship stances identified in the video, which one most resembles you on a bad day? Where do you think you learned this? How has it affected you in life? How has it affected others? Is this stance in danger of becoming your permanent role or "brand" in relationships? If that happens, do you see yourself getting happier or more alone?

_____

_____

_____

_____

6 What if you still want to do a behavior and aren't ready to give it up? What if God, your spouse, and others all think of it as unwanted, but you still think it's not that bad? What if you are convinced it isn't anyone's business but yours, and you're still doing fine? What usually happens in such scenarios? Who are you willing to listen to in such a moment? Are you willing to let the members of this group speak truth to you?

_____

_____

_____

_____

_____

_____

_____

_____

_____

Read and Reflect

It is for freedom that Christ has set us free. Stand firm, then, and do

not let yourselves be burdened again by a yoke of slavery.

—Galatians 5:1

Read this passage three or four times, either silently as individuals or out loud as a group. What is its message? Consider committing part or all of this passage to memory over the next week.

Respond

This session explained the concept of unwanted behaviors and gave you some categories to use when identifying them and sorting out when they started. What is one big lesson that jumps out in your heart as a matter for prayer and reflection so far, and/or what is one specific action you can commit to try between this session and the next?

Pray

Close your group time by praying in any of the following directions:

- Pray that God will help you and those around you to make an honest assessment of your unwanted behaviors this week.
- Pray that you can learn to want *all* of your behaviors to match God's boundaries in terms of both morality and scope. Ask the Holy Spirit to show you if any of your behaviors have gone out of control into unhealthy coping.
- Pray for people affected by the unwanted behaviors of another. Ask that God will defend them, protect them, and give them patience, wisdom, and grace until healing comes.
- Ask God to give you another breakthrough moment this week, where some of your unwanted patterns show signs of weakening in response to prayer and God's work in your heart.

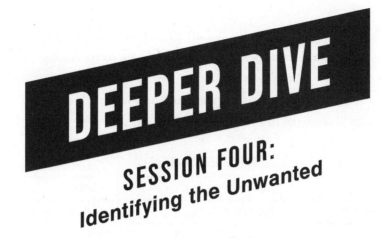

DEEPER DIVE

SESSION FOUR:
Identifying the Unwanted

UNHEALTHY ATTEMPTS TO COPE

Read . . .

My friend, therapist Jay Stringer, has done a lot of work and research on unwanted behaviors, which he defines as any behavior that, at the end of the day, we wish was not a part of our lives. Similarly, we define unwanted behaviors as any compulsive thought, belief, or action you want to stop but can't.

You may have unmet longings in your life that contribute to some unwanted behaviors. Perhaps you've thought, "People aren't safe, and they will reject me," and you can't seem to shake it. Maybe you harbor a belief that you are not lovable, despite what others tell you. Perhaps you're like 46 percent of Americans who report feeling alone, or like the 47 percent who feel left out.[*] Or maybe you struggle with consistent obsessive thoughts or actions about money, your appearance, or material things. Maybe you battle depression.

You may have tried different ways of coping with lingering hurts springing from unmet needs. Maybe you try to cope with your uncomfortable emotions by over-eating or smoking weed. Perhaps you immerse yourself in TV watching to numb

---

[*] Multivu, "New Cigna Study Reveals Loneliness at Epidemic Levels in America," May 1, 2018, http://www.multivu.com/players/English/8294451-cigna-us-loneliness-survey/.

your pain.* Maybe you spend money you don't have or go on shopping sprees to distract you from facing the hard-to-deal-with emotions. Maybe you're among the 91 percent of men and 62 percent of women who turn to pornography.† The following is a list of common unwanted behaviors we can get stuck in. Can you identify any coping behaviors that hold you back from the life of wholeness God has for you?

COPING BEHAVIOR TABLE

Adultery	Alcohol(ism)	Anger/Rage
Anxiety/Fear/Worry	Approval of Others	Boasting/Bragging
Body Image Issues	Cheating/Cutting Corners	Complaining
Control	Depression	Disobedience/Rebellion
Divorce/Separation	Drugs/Substance Abuse/Pills	Fantasy
Fear of Failure	Fear of Intimacy	Gambling
Greed	Hopelessness	Insecurity
Isolation/Withdrawal	Jealousy/Envy	Lack of Growth
Laziness	Lying/Deceit/Dishonesty	Materialism
Overeating/Undereating	Oversleeping/Undersleeping	Overspending
Overworking	Perfectionism	Poor Boundaries
Pornography/Arousing Images or Writing	Pride/Self-Righteousness/Judgmentalism	Procrastination
Profanity/Swearing/Cursing	Racism	Resentment/Bitterness
Self-Harm/Cutting	Self-Sabotage	Self-Worth/Too High or Too Low
Sexual Compulsivity	Smoking/Dipping/Vaping	Social Media
Stealing	Streaming Media (Netflix, YouTube, etc.)	Suicidal Thoughts
Unforgiveness	Unhealthy Relationships	Victim Mentality
Video Games		**Total:**

---

* Alexis C. Madrigal, "When Did TV Watching Peak?" *The Atlantic*, May 30, 2018, http://www.theatlantic.com/technology/archive/2018/05/when-did-tv-watching-peak/561464/.

† Ingrid Solano, Nicholas R. Eaton, and K. Daniel O'Leary, "Pornography Consumption, Modality and Function in a Large Internet Sample." *Journal of Sex Research* 57, no. 1 (January 2020): 92–103, https://doi.org/10.1080/00224499.2018.1532488.

Assess...

1 What was the total number of individual coping behaviors from the chart that you have struggled with?

_____

_____

_____

2 What stance(s) have you found yourself occupying in relationships with others?

_____

_____

_____

3 What are your top three unwanted behaviors that you still struggle with, and when did each behavior begin in your life?

_____

_____

_____

4 In relationships, what effect does the stance(s) you take have on you and the other person (or people)?

_____

_____

_____

SESSION FIVE

LISTEN TO YOUR LONGINGS

WELCOME

If you drive a vehicle, you know that it has gauges and lights intended to tell us important things about how the vehicle is doing along the way. We all hope to buy a vehicle that never flashes a "check engine" light or suddenly registers a high water temperature. In fact, we so desire a maintenance-free vehicle that we get in the habit of ignoring the lights—that's why, in order to get our attention, manufacturers make these lights orange, yellow, or red. Living our lives without listening to our longings is like driving a vehicle and completely ignoring the gauges—we never know why our lives pull sharply to the side into unwanted behaviors (flat tire), why we are so tired (out of fuel), or why we are burning with such intense passions and pains (overheating).

This session will help you start to make a connection between the gauges (unmet longings) and the vehicle's problems (your unwanted behaviors). Once you realize that these unmet longings are actually messengers from the deep parts of your soul and your story, sent by God to get your attention and lead you to healing, joy, and freedom in him, the process starts to get both powerful and easier at the same time. Many people merely treat the symptoms, white-knuckling through their unwanted behaviors without ever understanding *why* they do what they do. Instead, you are going to join the chorus of witnesses who testify that Jesus has led them to unpack their past, learn their motives, and actually experience healing at the root of the problem.

SHARE

- How did the process of identifying your unmet longings and coping behaviors go? Did you find any longings and behaviors that surprised you or were hard to admit, or was the process predictable, based on what you already knew about yourself?
- As you look forward, how likely do you think you are to change much at this point in your life? Do you feel too old and stuck in your patterns, or do you believe you still have some growth potential in you? Is there hope of you experiencing new patterns and greater satisfaction?

WATCH

Play the video for *Session 5: Listen to Your Longings* from the *Free to Thrive Video Study*. As you watch, use the following outline to record any thoughts, questions, or key points that stand out to you.

- Ernie and Jackie's experience

_____

_____

_____

_____

Looking Back to Move Ahead

- Our past hurts and experiences have an impact on our present.

_____

_____

_____

• It's crucial to look back and realize how we got where we are.

_____

_____

_____

More Than Our Nature

• Our unwanted behaviors are certainly a product of being born with brokenness inside of us.

_____

_____

_____

_____

• It's not just us, though; most of our unwanted behaviors are responses to sins done to us and hurts we received.

_____

_____

_____

_____

• Until we understand the connection, we are likely to stay stuck. This process is not about making excuses or placing blame—it is about breaking cycles. You can't change what you don't understand.

_____

_____

_____

_____

Listen to Your Longings

• There is always a connection between our longings and our unwanted behaviors.

_____

_____

_____

- Han's story

  _____

  _____

  _____

- Fedel's experience (Anthony Flagg)

  _____

  _____

  _____

- This is a powerful process that requires patience with yourself.

  _____

  _____

  _____

DISCUSS

With your group, discuss what you have just watched and explore these concepts in Scripture. Use the following questions to guide your discussion.

1 As explored in this session, our unwanted behaviors aren't random; they're signals to be answered. They're signals for deeper longings. They're ways of seeking the fulfillment of our Seven Longings in unhealthy ways. Think back to session 4 where we discussed unwanted behaviors and the four relational stances. How might these struggles in your life be ways of attempting to fulfill one or more of the Seven Longings that have gone unmet through attacks and absences?

_____

_____

_____

_____

_____

2 **Read:** Genesis 50:15–21. In this passage, we see Joseph and his brothers reconciling after honestly addressing the hurts of the past between them. What about Joseph's response appeals to you? Does anything about it bother you? If looking into the past could help you sense God's good purposes more than the other's evil intent, what would this mean to you?

_____

_____

_____

_____

3 Can you already think of someone like Joseph's brothers who hurt you through attacks or absences? Maybe you have forgiven them—that's great! But their harmful actions may still be affecting you. Think of one of those hurts, and see if you can identify which of your Seven Longings were affected in that instance. If that longing left a mark on your heart, which of your unwanted behaviors might be an attempt to fulfill it? If none initially line up, do some more thinking—there's probably a connection somewhere.

_____

_____

_____

_____

4 Have you ever found yourself playing "whack-a-mole" with an old hurt that keeps popping up in different places through new unwanted behaviors and is continuing to cause problems? Share the example with the group, even if you haven't yet sorted out how it connects to your longings and current unwanted behaviors.

_____

_____

_____

_____

5 **Read:** Deuteronomy 15:12–18. In this passage, God gives instructions about setting indentured servants free rather than keeping them as slaves. The Israelites are told to remember their own past slavery as the basis for being generous in setting others free. Is this a principle you can apply? How might remembering your past hurts and slavery to unwanted behaviors actually set you free to be more generous to others? How might looking back help you love forward?

_____

_____

_____

_____

_____

6 Does understanding that unmet longings lie behind unwanted behaviors give you greater compassion for people in their struggles? How about when their unwanted behaviors directly impact you?

_____

_____

_____

_____

_____

Read and Reflect

The purposes of a person's heart are deep waters,

but one who has insight draws them out.

—Proverbs 20:5

Read this passage three or four times, either silently as individuals or out loud as a group. What is its message? Consider committing part or all of this passage to memory over the next week.

Respond

This session has challenged you to begin the hard detective work of linking your past experiences, hurts, and pains with your current unwanted behaviors. What is one big lesson that jumps out in your heart as a matter for prayer and reflection so far, and/or what is one specific action you can commit to try between this session and the next?

Pray

Close your group time by praying in any of the following directions:

- Pray that you will be given accurate and honest memories of your past as you do this work of listening to your longings.
- Ask God to help and protect any members of the group that express a reluctance to try this task; some of us require special protection and concern, which the group can offer in prayer and deed.
- Thank God for giving you gauges in your life to alert you to unresolved hurts and point you toward him.
- Pray for others out there who may be facing the same kinds of traumas and hurts you did. Ask God to show you how looking back and learning could help you protect them and make their experience better than yours was.

SESSION FIVE:
Listen to Your Longings

EMOTIONAL SIGNALS

Read . . .

Emotions help us to get in touch with what is going on inside of us. You may not think of yourself as an emotional person, but you are; we all are. Emotions are part of what it means to be human. We are all designed to feel deeply and to be aware of what is going on inside of us. We are created to experience happiness, gratitude, excitement, sadness, anger, disgust, trust, and peace. In this we are like our Creator, who experiences emotions himself. Scripture depicts God expressing joy (Zephaniah 3:17), peace (John 14:27), grief (John 11:35), anger (Psalm 103:8), and many more emotions. Experiencing emotions is part of what it means to be made in God's image.

So what do emotions have to do with our unwanted behaviors? Well, emotions give us insight into what is going on inside of us, into what we are longing for. Whenever we experience emotions, we are experiencing either the fulfillment or unfulfillment of one or more of the Seven Longings we discussed earlier. So we must learn to listen to our longings. When you find yourself giving in to an unwanted behavior, ask yourself, "Which of the Seven Longings am I seeking out in this unwanted behavior?" Think about what happened that day, the week before, and the month before. Think about what upcoming challenges you may be anticipating. What interactions with people caused your longings to go unmet? What circumstances in your life caused you to turn inward and start believing lies about yourself? What challenges have you faced that may have caused you to feel rejected, unsafe, or shameful? Was it being criticized by your boss, being left out by friends, or feeling overwhelmed with tasks to do? Was it feeling like a failure once again as you didn't measure up to your own expectations or someone else's? What longing might you have been fearing would go unmet in the future?

Assess . . .

1 Begin the practice of listening to your longings. Which of the Seven Longings might you be seeking out in your primary unwanted behaviors?

_____

_____

_____

2 In what recent ways through interactions with people, circumstances, and events have those longings gone unmet?

_____

_____

_____

3 What feelings and rewards are temporarily brought on by attempting to meet those unmet longings?

_____

_____

_____

_____

4 Why might this longing be of such significance for you? Where might this longing have gone unmet in your past?

_____

_____

_____

_____

SESSION SIX

WHAT YOUR BRAIN NEEDS YOU TO KNOW

WELCOME

After thinking about your unwanted behaviors and cataloguing them over the last few sessions, you have probably become aware of an area or two in which you feel less secure and steady than you would wish. If our unwanted behaviors teach us anything, they confirm that we are not yet as in control of ourselves and our feelings as we had hoped. In fact, they show us that there are patterns and systems at work in us, without our full awareness, that have the capacity to redirect our intentions and produce unanticipated fruit. This realization can be alarming!

This all plainly proves that there are things happening under the surface in our minds that can trap us in dissatisfaction and pain. Such things, if left unattended, can lead to toxic beliefs and behaviors that may overwhelm us with unexpected loneliness or despair. To understand how this happens, we need to explore the way our brains work and how repeated thoughts, experiences, and behaviors affect our minds. Once we do this, we will discover that although a battle is raging for our minds, God has given us tools to win the fight and take back lost ground. Today's session will engage in this process as we strive to unpack the way our brains are wired—and can be rewired—to change our beliefs and behaviors.

SHARE

- Last week, we explored the connection between our unmet longings and unwanted behaviors. Did you have any discoveries throughout the week about why you might do certain things you don't want to do? Did you discover any unmet longings you seek to fulfill through unwanted behaviors?
- Tell your group about a time when you caught yourself thinking wrongly and how those thoughts had been affecting you before you noticed they were distorted.

WATCH

Play the video for *Session 6: What Your Brain Needs You to Know* from the *Free to Thrive Video Study*. As you watch, use the following outline to record any thoughts, questions, or key points that stand out to you.

When Our Beliefs Catch Up to Us

- More of Ben's story

_____

_____

_____

_____

_____

_____

_____

_____

_____

Blaming vs. Naming

- It is essential that we name and properly weigh our past experiences and the default patterns they have helped create in us.

_____

_____

_____

The Battle of the Brain

- Our behavior follows our beliefs.

_____

_____

_____

- The limbic system vs. the rational brain

_____

_____

_____

- Audrey's experience

_____

_____

_____

- Ernie and Jackie's experience

_____

_____

_____

Behavior Follows Belief

- Nate's story

_____

_____

_____

- Over time our experiences, thoughts, and choices cause a physical change in our brains.

  _____

  _____

  _____

Hope for Your Brain

- Renewing of the mind and "neuroplasticity"

  _____

  _____

  _____

- Over time, we can collaboratively work with the Holy Spirit to develop new neurological pathways.

  _____

  _____

  _____

DISCUSS

With your group, discuss what you have just watched and explore these concepts in Scripture. Use the following questions to guide your discussion.

1 There is an old saying in philosophy, "I think, therefore I am." This session is making the point that we can also say, "I think, therefore I feel and do." What is your reaction to this session's teaching about our behaviors following our beliefs? Does that make sense and match your experience?

_____

_____

_____

_____

_____

2 **Read:** 2 Corinthians 10:3–5. Ben quoted this passage in the session video. Take some time to think more deeply about the passage. Can you give an example of "a pretension that sets itself up against the knowledge of God"? Can you share any personal examples of experiences that led to unhealthy beliefs or thoughts about God, yourself, or others?

_____

_____

_____

_____

3 As you think about some of the thoughts and pretensions which have interfered with your progress in the knowledge of God and his ways for your life, where did they mostly come from? Were they taught to you, and by whom? Were they in media or popular culture? Were they vows you made after a negative experience? Are they still there and in need of demolition?

_____

_____

_____

_____

4 **Read:** Psalm 13. Can you find any evidence in this psalm that its writer was fighting the battle for the mind? What kinds of enemies do you imagine are being talked about? What kinds of enemies would you be thinking of if this psalm were about your story? What spiritual weapons for demolishing does the psalmist decide to use? Do you think this strategy would also work for you?

_____

_____

_____

_____

5 What is an area of your childhood where neurons fired together until they wired together due to repeated unhealthy beliefs and behaviors? Said differently, what experiences led to negative core beliefs and what repeated patterns of thoughts and unwanted behaviors resulted? For example: Did the challenges of schoolwork or sports lead to thoughts of inadequacy and a pattern of shaming yourself? Did hurtful words or actions from friends lead to feelings of rejection and hiding your internal life or consistent anxiety? Did a lack of attention or being misunderstood by family lead to feeling alone and a pattern of unhealthy relationships?

_____

_____

_____

_____

_____

6 How do you think these fixed neurological pathways might be playing out today?

_____

_____

_____

_____

7 **Read:** Romans 12:2. How does knowing that your brain's fixed pathways of thoughts, beliefs, and actions can be rewired (neuroplasticity) impact you? Does knowing that certain things in your life can actually change and get better give you relief?

_____

_____

_____

_____

Read and Reflect

> Do not conform to the pattern of this world, but be
>
> transformed by the renewing of your mind.
>
> —Romans 12:2

Read this passage three or four times, either silently as individuals or out loud as a group. What is its message? Consider committing part or all of this passage to memory over the next week.

Respond

This session focused on the way our beliefs lead to behaviors and the role we are called to play in curating our own minds. What is one big lesson that jumps out in your heart as a matter for prayer and reflection so far, and/or what is one specific action you can commit to try between this session and the next?

Pray

Close your group time by praying in any of the following directions:

- Pray that God will help you to spot faulty thoughts and beliefs more easily and clearly. Invite him to illuminate your mind and help you sort it.
- Use the spiritual weapons God has given you in prayer—say things like, "I reject in the name of Jesus the false belief that my worth comes from external beauty" or "I refuse to let unforgiveness ruin my happiness—I release my anger toward _____ in Jesus's name."
- Pray for the courage to name experiences and teachings that led to false beliefs in you without any guilt or feelings of disloyalty. You aren't blaming others—you are simply acknowledging what is broken in your life and how it got that way.
- Thank God for the wonderful way he has constructed our brains and for knowing us so well that he can help us heal them, no matter what has been done by us or to us.

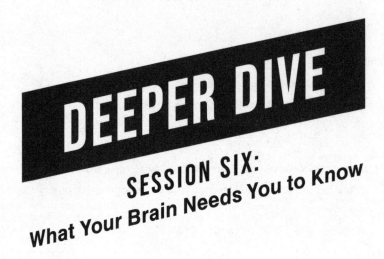

DEEPER DIVE

SESSION SIX:
What Your Brain Needs You to Know

BEHAVIOR FOLLOWS BELIEF

Read . . .

As we go throughout our lives, the lies we believe are triggered by our circumstances. Your boyfriend or girlfriend breaks up with you. Your boss criticizes you. An overwhelming task is handed to you. A friend disagrees with you. The kids refuse to listen to you. Your longings go unmet—again—and those unmet longings trigger your negative core beliefs. They feel so real and true in the moment. When this happens, you want to escape the stress and pain as quickly as possible; you want to feel better. You attempt to have your longings met in an unhealthy way.

A few years ago, I (Ben) was mentoring a college student, and as we started to talk about his life growing up, he shared how he often didn't feel accepted for who he was. He felt like he couldn't measure up to his parents' expectations. His grades were never up to their standards. His parents said he was too emotional. He struggled to fit in with his friends. He had a deep longing to be accepted for who he was—a need that often went unmet. As we talked week after week about the recent times he became angry or the times he went to porn, sure enough, there was always an incident right before these instances that left him feeling rejected or inadequate. He had been caught in this cycle for years. His anger and porn use were ways for him to feel in control, attempt to protect himself, and receive a hit of dopamine.

The following diagram is an attempt to visually explain this cycle, representing how circumstances in our present-day life can trigger our unmet longings and negative core beliefs, leading us back to our unwanted behaviors.

UNWANTED BEHAVIOR CYCLE

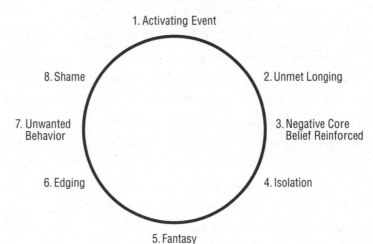

1. Activating Event
8. Shame
2. Unmet Longing
7. Unwanted Behavior
3. Negative Core Belief Reinforced
6. Edging
4. Isolation
5. Fantasy

1. **Activating Event.** A situation or circumstance that produces in you—consciously or subconsciously—an awareness of your need. Someone hurts you, you were anticipating a reward or pleasure that didn't happen, or you didn't perform a task as well as you had hoped. There are countless activating events in our daily lives, all of which are unique to our personal stories.

2. **Unmet Longing.** When we experience an activating event, we feel the pain of one or more of our Seven Longings going unmet. We may not recognize the unmet need, but we experience the pain.

3. **Negative Core Belief Reinforced.** When we experience an unmet longing, it triggers or reinforces the negative core beliefs and lies we believe, carving the pathway in the brain a little deeper and affirming the lies that have already taken root.

4. **Isolation.** Next, our tendency is to separate, even isolate, ourselves from other people and situations that (in our minds, at least) may maintain or increase

our pain. Rather than dealing with what is going on inside of us, we ignore it or try to outrun it.

5. **Fantasy.** Trying to escape the unmet longing, situations, and core lies leads us to a fantasy world. We start thinking about what we could have said or done differently. We check out of reality and begin thinking about going to our unwanted behaviors. We then start plotting how to go down the path again to these behaviors.

6. **Edging.** We flirt with the idea of giving in to the cravings. "I'll just have one beer." "I'll just take a look." "I know I shouldn't, but just this once." We edge closer to the line we swore we'd never cross again.

7. **Unwanted Behavior.** We give in once more to an unwanted behavior, slipping into a rut we've traveled many times before. We may think we just ended up there suddenly because we weren't strong enough or the temptation surprised us, but in reality we took a predictable—and preventable—path to get there.

8. **Shame.** The cycle leads inevitably to shame. Our unmet longings were never truly satisfied. The core lies are further reinforced. The unwanted behaviors are repeated, and we are as vulnerable as before to repeating the entire cycle the next time an activating event occurs.

Assess . . .

1 What negative core beliefs about yourself might you have developed from your unmet longings?

_____

_____

_____

_____

2 What negative core beliefs about God might you have developed from your unmet longings?

_____

_____

_____

_____

3 What negative core beliefs about others might you have developed from your unmet longings?

_____

_____

_____

_____

4 What are two or three common activating events in your life that lead to unmet longings and reinforce some of these negative core beliefs?

_____

_____

_____

_____

YOU'VE GOT THE WRONG GOD

WELCOME

It makes sense—when we can't see God with our eyes, we tend to fill in the blanks with things we've already seen. We create a version of God that is really a projection of our hopes, fears, biases, and experiences. The problem with these projections is that they aren't the *real* God. And our hearts are too hungry to be satisfied by anything less than the *real* God. These lesser "gods" we invent tend to reinforce our pains, false beliefs, and thoughts until we are sparring with our own worst fears and stuck places, supposedly in the name of our God.

So how do we break this cycle? We can only be truly happy when we are in a thriving, honest, and dynamic relationship with the one and only living God, with ourselves, and with God's people. He loves us too much to let us be satisfied with less. This session will help us begin to peel back the layers of our perception of God until we see the true God revealed in the Bible and in the person and work of Jesus Christ.

SHARE

- Can you think of something cute or funny you used to think about God when you were little? When did you realize that this was not accurate? How do you understand things now?

- Have you ever been in a situation where you noticed someone was relating to a made-up version of you? Maybe a boyfriend or girlfriend thought you were more perfect than you are in real life, or maybe a coworker was fighting against a much meaner and scarier version of you than you felt was fair? Did you ever get them to see the real you? How did it feel being misunderstood like that? Have you ever thought about God feeling that way?

WATCH

Play the video for _Session 7: You've Got the Wrong God_ from the _Free to Thrive Video Study_. As you watch, use the following outline to record any thoughts, questions, or key points that stand out to you.

When God _Seems_ to Disappoint

- Ben's loss of his friend Alex made him feel angry at God. That anger was really an expression of his fear that God might not be as good as he thought.

_____

_____

_____

_____

Do You Have the Wrong God?

- Sometimes our experiences and beliefs have wired in a false idea of God.

_____

_____

_____

_____

- Monica's experience

We All Have Daddy Issues
- Earthly authority figures can deeply affect our perception of God.

What If God Isn't Who You Think?
- If you are a Christian, God isn't angry with you—he loves you as much as he loves his perfect Son, Jesus, in whom you now stand.

- Ernie and Jackie's experience

- God is not obsessed with rules nor uptight—he is gracious and forgiving.

- God isn't distant and disconnected—he is present, personal, and intervening in your life right now.

_____

_____

_____

_____

You Can See God as He Truly Is

- God loves us and wants to show us himself fully and accurately. We have a greater Father who can overcome our "daddy issues."

_____

_____

_____

_____

DISCUSS

With your group, discuss what you have just watched and explore these concepts in Scripture. Use the following questions to guide your discussion.

1 What do you picture in your mind when you imagine God? What art, iconography, movies, or mental images come to mind? What about when you picture Jesus? More to the point, what attributes come to mind when you think of God—not theological traits so much, but personality traits? Who is he? What is he like? Where did you get these ideas?

_____

_____

_____

_____

_____

_____

2 Reflect as a group on some of the things this session assured us that God is NOT (angry, uptight, distant). Be honest: which of these have you been tempted to believe about God? Are there other false images or reputations you have struggled with so far in your pursuit of God? What negative experiences with authority figures might have led you to view God harshly? How can your group help you to name those negative attributes, think about them in light of Scripture, and sort them out a little better?

_____

_____

_____

_____

3 **Read:** Psalm 68:5–6. This passage mentions profound ways that God shows his goodness, love, and care to his people. What are some things this passage reveals about God's nature? What does it reveal about his heart toward you?

_____

_____

_____

_____

4 **Read:** Isaiah 65:1–16. This passage gives us a first-person sense of what God feels when people worship a false or twisted version of him. What do you notice about God's frustration in this passage? What about his mercy, patience, and desire to be known fully, even when people are misunderstanding him? How does it feel to think about it from his perspective?

_____

_____

_____

_____

5 How do you think we can know we are the "servants" described in the previous passage? What traits and fruits might assure us that we are on God's side (by his grace) and that we are responding to him in a way that pleases and honors him? What would it look like to be the people that are opposed to God and described as "smoke in [his] nostrils"?

_____

_____

_____

_____

_____

6 **Read:** 1 John 3:1–3. This passage is meant to increase your desire to think of God properly and worship him as he truly is. After all, if we don't understand who God really is, how can we know what we are living into? This world not only fails to fully see God as he is, but it also fails to see us believers as we truly are. This passage talks about a day when we will no longer worship the wrong God, nor will Christians be misunderstood and rejected. What kinds of revelations do you imagine when you read this passage? If we become like what we worship, what can we expect when following Jesus over a lifetime?

_____

_____

_____

_____

Read and Reflect

> You will seek me and find me when you seek me with all your heart.
>
> —Jeremiah 29:13

Read this passage three or four times, either silently as individuals or out loud as a group. What is its message? Consider committing part or all of this passage to memory over the next week.

Respond

This session was aimed at helping you notice and debunk any false perceptions of God you may have picked up along the way in life. What is one big lesson that jumps out in your heart as a matter for prayer and reflection so far, and/or what is one specific action you can commit to try between this session and the next?

Pray

Close your group time by praying in any of the following directions:

- Pray to God and ask him to help you spot and tear down any warped or false versions of him in your heart. Confess any misunderstanding you find and name the place it came from, if you can.
- Ask God to convict the members of your group regarding the three basic beliefs about him we studied in this session: his kindness, his forgiveness, and his presence.
- Thank God for loving us and his own glory too much to put up with false images of himself.
- Willingly forgive (out loud in prayer) anyone who gave you a false perception of God, whether he or she knew it or not.

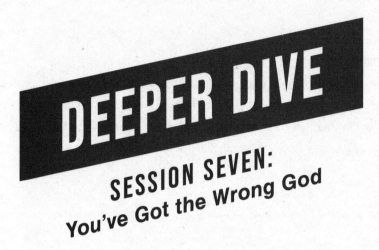

SESSION SEVEN:
You've Got the Wrong God

GUT CHECK ON GOD

Read . . .

If you're questioning whether or not you have wrong perceptions about God, here are some common examples of what these beliefs and actions can look like. These may not be conscious thoughts, but are negative core beliefs deep within our hearts and minds that bear fruit in our actions:

- I do good things to try to earn the love and acceptance of God.
- I often worry about the future, my safety, and finances, doubting God's provision.
- I feel like God is distant from me when I sin and is waiting for me to get my life together.
- I think God is often disappointed in me.
- I believe God loves me but doesn't really like me. He just tolerates me.
- I think God loves me more when I perform, do good, or fulfill religious duties.
- I think God is obsessed with rules and regulations.
- I believe God is consistently angry with me due to my choices.
- I think God isn't going to be there when I need him the most.
- I think God couldn't possibly forgive me or love me after what I've done.

Wherever you are in your journey, we invite you to consider implementing some of the following steps that God has used to help us continue to grow in seeing and experiencing God for who he truly is, being transformed by the renewing of our minds.

- Regularly remembering what God has done in your life
- Talking to him throughout the day
- Daily thanking him for five good things he did or gave you that day
- Reading the Bible through the lens of who God truly is as a loving and engaging Father
- Looking for the good gifts, the subtle things, that are his love and kindness to you
- Reading books by authors who see God as he truly is
- Listening to teachers and preachers who teach from the Scriptures and have an emphasis on who we are as his beloved, cherished, righteous sons and daughters
- Meditating daily on who God is as your loving Father
- Hanging out with people who model God's love and engagement to you
- Getting to know and observing loving fathers who are engaging with their kids
- Being quick to take wrong thoughts about God captive and reminding yourself who he actually is
- Identifying and working through the negative experiences, wrong messages, and unmet longings you have from past experiences with your father, authority figures, and/or spiritual teachers
- Identifying the practical ways God has and is (directly and through other people in your life) currently meeting your Seven Longings

Assess...

1 What negative core beliefs might you have about God?

_____

_____

_____

_____

_____

_____

2 What unmet longings, painful experiences, or past relationships with authority figures might have contributed to these beliefs?

_____

_____

_____

_____

3 What one positive core belief about who God truly is do you want to develop?

_____

_____

_____

_____

4 What fathers in your life model well who God truly is, so that you can intentionally learn from them?

_____

_____

_____

_____

SESSION EIGHT

SEEING YOURSELF AS GOD SEES YOU

WELCOME

Have you ever been mistaken about how you look from the outside? Maybe you thought your outfit was great, until you noticed a tear in your pants when passing a mirror. Maybe you thought you were dancing like a pro, until you saw your moves on video. Perhaps you thought you were making a great impression, until someone told you there was broccoli in your teeth. In all of these cases, we may feel a cringe or shock to find ourselves coming across as *less* smooth and polished than we had hoped. These examples relate to a disconnect between how we thought we appeared versus what transpired. Similarly, we all deal with a disconnect between our thoughts and beliefs about ourselves on the inside versus how God views us.

Too often, our wrong views about God also link to incorrect ideas about who we are and how he sees us. We can buy into lies about ourselves, our potential in God's hands, our future security and hope, and even the possibility of receiving divine love. But what would it feel like to learn that we are *more* lovable, accepted, and valuable than we had ever hoped? This session is aimed at helping you piece together a biblical and sustainable sense of your worth, identity, and value according to the Word of God and the gospel it unveils. What matters is seeing ourselves the way God does and neither adding to it nor taking away from it—we pray this session helps you zero in on that.

SHARE

- Can you remember a time when you did not have an accurate perception of yourself from the outside, or do you know someone else struggling with this? What kinds of challenges did the situation include? Why could the person not see it? Who clued the blinded person in? How did he or she react?
- On a scale from 0–10, how comfortable are you with the idea that God loves you and has endowed you with special worth? In other words, how easily can you accept the idea that God likes you and wants to make much of you? Whether your answer runs low or high, where did you learn that perspective? How hard (or delightful) do you predict this lesson will be for you?

WATCH

Play the video for _Session 8: Seeing Yourself as God Sees You_ from the *Free to Thrive Video Study*. As you watch, use the following outline to record any thoughts, questions, or key points that stand out to you.

Skewing Negative

- All the hurt and unmet longings we've experienced can lead to negative beliefs about ourselves.

_____

_____

_____

_____

_____

A Case of Mistaken Identity

- Ever since the fall of humans, shame has left us tempted to hide from God and to think of ourselves as bad or not good enough at the core of our being.

_____

_____

_____

_____

_____

- Monica's experience

_____

_____

_____

_____

_____

Your True Identity

- A healthy self-image is seeing yourself as God sees you—no more and no less. Let's take a look at how he sees us:
  - **You are of great value:** You are so infinitely valuable that God gave his only Son to reconcile you to himself, paying an incalculable ransom.

  _____

  _____

  _____

  _____

  - **You are lovable:** God doesn't merely tolerate you—he loves you, he likes you, and he wanted you so much that he gave everything for you.

  _____

  _____

  _____

  _____

○ **You are unique:** You display God's image in a way no one else can or ever will.

_____

_____

_____

- Fedel's experience (Anthony Flagg)

_____

_____

_____

_____

Becoming Who You Already Are

- Our God-given identity is true and assured; however, it takes intentionality to live into who we are. We are called to live into—more and more each day—the people God created us to be.

DISCUSS

With your group, discuss what you have just watched and explore these concepts in Scripture. Use the following questions to guide your discussion.

1 The video from this session talks about our inner portrait and distinguishes between accurate, biblical views of who we are versus distorted ones. What is your inner portrait like? What are some of the good things you see there? What are some of the painful things you see there? What does God have to say about each? Do your fellow group members seem to resonate with the portrait you shared?

_____

_____

_____

_____

2 Shame can disguise itself as what we think is humility in our lives. Why do you think some Christians mistake humility as a low view of self? What do you think humility should look like in light of the profound love and worth God has given us?

_____

_____

_____

_____

_____

3 **Read:** Zephaniah 3:17. How does this promise of God's presence and lavish affection to you match (or not match) the inner portrait you shared? On what basis does the Lord promise to rejoice over us? Is it on our performance, or on his own accord alone? If it is the latter, can anything diminish or reduce it?

_____

_____

_____

_____

_____

4 This session clarifies that while it is important to our salvation to admit that we are born sinners, our sense of identity is not supposed to stay in this place. We need to gratefully and humbly identify now as new creations, saints, and sheep of Christ's own sheepfold. Have you stopped thinking of yourself as a sinner and now identified as a new creation—a saint who struggles with sin? If not, how do you think this new identity would impact your view of yourself and your relationship with God and others?

_____

_____

_____

_____

_____

5 **Read:** Psalm 103. Take time to think through the messages of comfort and understanding in this psalm. What jumps out at you as you read it? What characteristics
of God are shared, and how do they increase your confidence and excitement in
the identity he has given you? In which ways does the psalmist insist that God is
exactly the right kind of God to love and transform sinners into saints? How might
this psalm also lead us to treat one another differently?

_____

_____

_____

_____

_____

_____

_____

_____

6 Imagine two married couples—one just celebrated their fiftieth anniversary, and the
other just made their vows and are leaving the altar. Regardless of the length they
have been married, their behaviors, or their experiences together, neither couple
is more married or less married. Similarly, our spiritual activity and behaviors will
never change our spiritual identity as Christians. That is, we will not be more of a
Christian or less of a Christian by anything we do or don't do. From the moment
of salvation our identity is saint, not sinner. We cannot do good things to get God
to love us any more than he already does. How does this truth affect the way you
view yourself? How might it affect you when you are struggling with unwanted
behaviors?

_____

_____

_____

_____

_____

_____

_____

Read and Reflect

> Therefore, if anyone is in Christ, the new creation has
> come: The old has gone, the new is here!
> —2 Corinthians 5:17

Read this passage three or four times, either silently as individuals or out loud as a group. What is its message? Consider committing part or all of this passage to memory over the next week.

Respond

This session focused on helping you to accept and bask in the identity God has graciously given you, so that you do not keep holding on to a distorted self-understanding. What is one big lesson that jumps out in your heart as a matter for prayer and reflection so far, and/or what is one specific action you can commit to try between this session and the next?

Pray

Close your group time by praying in any of the following directions:

- Pray for any people in the group who shared a struggle with their inner portrait. Pray that they will see themselves the way God sees them—pray Scripture over them and share passages that will strengthen a biblical self-understanding.
- Pray for people (in your group or in the world) in the midst of verbal, emotional, physical, or sexual abuse/neglect. Pray that they will reject any false messages about their worth and identity.
- Confess any false identities—negative or positive—you are tempted to cling to rather than to what Christ says about you. Ask God to show you yourself properly—neither more highly nor more harshly than he does.
- Ask the Lord to give you both true humility and confidence to think of yourself accurately.

DEEPER DIVE

SESSION EIGHT:
Seeing Yourself as God Sees You

WORTHLESS? UNLOVABLE?

Read . . .

People with a clear view of their true identity feel significant. They understand that they matter to God and to others, and that the world is a better place because they are here. They are able to interact with others and appreciate their worth without feeling threatened. They radiate hope, joy, and trust because they are secure in their identity as God's children. They accept themselves as lovable, worthy, and competent members of God's creation, redeemed and reconciled to God to become all he wants them to be.

However, those with a cloudy view of their identity as God's creation display a number of debilitating traits. The most common ways a clouded identity manifests itself is through the negative core beliefs of being worthless, unlovable, or just a face in the crowd. You may believe that you are worthless, that God simply tolerates you, or that he loves you but doesn't really like you. Maybe you wouldn't put it just that way, but ask yourself if you identify with any of the statements in the following list:

- ☐ I don't know or truly believe what God says about my true value
- ☐ I find myself hustling and striving for a sense of worth
- ☐ I obsess about my physical appearance, personality, and what people think

☐ I often fear rejection

☐ I worry about people abandoning me

☐ I am embarrassed easily

☐ I often feel inadequate, incapable, or not good enough

☐ I feel sad about myself at times

☐ I find myself trying to prove my value through success, name dropping, approval of others, or material possessions

☐ I struggle with procrastination

☐ I greatly fear failure

☐ I neglect my emotional and physical needs

More specifically, you may have had unmet longings and experiences that have led you to believe you were unlovable. Consider how this negative core belief may be manifested in your life by asking yourself if you identify with any of the statements in the following list:

☐ I fear what other people will say or do in response to my thoughts or actions

☐ I struggle with people-pleasing or doing whatever it takes to "keep the peace" with others

☐ I think if people really knew me—or what I've done—they'd reject me

☐ I struggle with anger

☐ I get very sad or angry when I feel left out

☐ I'm afraid of being fully known

☐ I struggle to open up about how I'm really feeling

☐ I can be overly sensitive and get hurt easily

☐ I feel like I'm a burden to people and a drain on their time

☐ I don't like who I am and struggle to love myself

☐ I don't like or love aspects of myself—physical traits, personality traits, etc.

Many of us can feel like we're just a number, a face in the crowd. Just one of seven-billion-some humans walking this earth, not much different than the next individual. We can hear things like "God created us" or "Jesus died on the cross for our sins and wants a personal relationship with us" and yet not receive them as personal and specific to us. We may think God created us, sure, but more or less like products of a factory assembly line rather than being involved in the fine details of uniquely wiring and gifting us. We may wonder about our significance and if it really matters whether or not we're here. Consider how this negative core belief may be manifest in your life by asking yourself if you identify with any of the statements in the following list:

- ☐ I believe that Jesus died for all, but wouldn't have died just for me
- ☐ I struggle with my purpose and direction in life
- ☐ I seldom think much about myself and my needs
- ☐ I struggle with motivation
- ☐ I don't see how the world is a better place because I'm here
- ☐ I don't think people care that I'm alive
- ☐ I don't see my unique contribution to this world
- ☐ I don't think I'm unique, gifted, and here to make an impact on the world

Assess . . .

1 Do you at times view yourself as either worthless, unlovable, or just a face in the crowd?

_____

_____

_____

_____

_____

2 What unmet longings and painful experiences from the past may have led you to develop those negative core beliefs about yourself?

_____

_____

_____

_____

_____

3 What positive core belief(s) about your true identity do you want to grow in believing?

_____

_____

_____

_____

_____

4 Do you know anyone with whom you can intentionally spend time—someone who treats you as valuable, loved, and unique?

_____

_____

_____

_____

_____

SESSION NINE

YOU'RE MADE FOR MORE

WELCOME

We need to feel and hear God's love and acceptance of us here on earth. He has given us his Word and his sacraments, but he never intended these to be all we need—we need other believing people to sharpen and support us! If you have been trying to do the Christian life alone, you have doubtless run into the truth contained in this session: you were *never meant to go it alone*, or to renew your mind without Christian brothers and sisters to help you. Hopefully, this study group is beginning to be an encouraging support for you, making a significant dent in any loneliness, stuckness, and unmet longings you may have.

God doesn't just want to save us *from* death, sin, and hell—he also wants to save us *for* something and *with* someone. He wants to save us into restored and thriving relationships with himself and his people. If you aren't yet sure if you have a cohort of authentic, sincere partners for support and growth, this session will challenge you to become vulnerable, ask for help, and offer yourself to others as a significant resource for maturing and learning. This may feel like a risk, but you can't thrive without community.

SHARE

- During the last session, we talked a lot about identity. How have you been growing in your identity since we last talked? Has God shown you anything new? Share your findings with the group.
- How much alone time do you need? Are you getting enough of it at this point in your life? How much together time do you need, and how is that going? Share your perceived need for people on a scale from 0–10, and then share the availability and quality of your current relationships on that same scale. Are you running on a deficit or a surplus? How are you coping with that reality?

WATCH

Play the video for *Session 9: You're Made for More* from the *Free to Thrive Video Study*. As you watch, use the following outline to record any thoughts, questions, or key points that stand out to you.

Searching for Connection

- More of Ben's story

_____

_____

_____

_____

How We Thrive

- Relational wholeness is what furthers and supports our spiritual and emotional wholeness.

_____

_____

_____

_____

- Fedel's experience (Anthony Flagg)

_____

_____

_____

_____

Relational Wholeness from a Relational God

- The first crisis in the Bible was the aloneness of Adam; God created him with a need for deep relationship with another human.

_____

_____

_____

- The New Testament contains 100 one-another passages that teach us about living out our faith in community.

_____

_____

_____

Human Connection: Surviving and Thriving

- The "Still Face Experiment" showed how much we are hardwired to depend on connection with others.

_____

_____

_____

Relational Brokenness and Wholeness

- No thriving person is isolated and disconnected, and no isolated and disconnected person is thriving.

_____

_____

_____

- "Vulnerability is the birthplace of love, belonging, joy, courage, empathy, and creativity" (Brené Brown).

_____

_____

_____

_____

_____

Growth Environments

- We need to find environments that foster spiritual, emotional, and relational growth and wholeness. These are places where:
    - . . . the truth about God and your value is clearly taught from the Scriptures.

    _____

    _____

    _____

    _____

    - . . . people experientially and relationally model the truth about who you are in Christ.

    _____

    _____

    _____

    _____

- Monica's experience

_____

_____

_____

_____

God's Plan for Your Growth

- We need a daily lifestyle of processing our emotions, stress, and pain with a couple of safe people.

  _____

  _____

  _____

- When we encounter a situation in which a longing goes unmet (an "activating event"):
  - Identify the unmet longing you are feeling

    _____

    _____

  - Acknowledge the God-given longing that underlies that sensation

    _____

    _____

  - Counter any negative core beliefs you may be telling yourself with the truth

    _____

    _____

  - Seek fulfillment of that longing in healthy ways
    - Call or text a friend to share what you're struggling through and ask him or her to affirm your identity

      _____

      _____

    - Talk to God and tell him the same things

      _____

      _____

  - Repeat as needed . . .

    _____

    _____

DISCUSS

With your group, discuss what you have just watched and explore these concepts in Scripture. Use the following questions to guide your discussion.

1 How comfortable are you with the idea that you need other people? This session is insisting that you are made for community, but some people strongly object to this part of God's plan for them. Are you eager for deeper relationships, or leery? Why do you think you feel this way? How can the members of this group help?

_____

_____

_____

_____

_____

_____

_____

_____

2 **Read:** Genesis 2:4–25. Were you shocked to hear that the first crisis in the Bible was *not* the fall and sin's arrival into our world? How can there have been something "not good" before there was sin? When God looks at your current portfolio of relationships, is he saying, "Very good," "Good start, but go deeper," or "It is not good for you to be this alone"?

_____

_____

_____

_____

_____

_____

_____

_____

3 The Still Face Experiment described in this session gives striking proof that human interaction is formative and essential for infants. How much healthy human contact have you received up to this point in your life? As you name the situations and people involved (avoid blaming, if you can) and take stock of your formation so far, what kinds of healing and help might you require from God? From others?

_____

_____

_____

_____

4 **Read:** Psalm 133. What does this passage seem to say about Spirit-led community and fellowship? How do the word pictures affect you? Mount Hermon is high and snow-capped, while Mount Zion is low and arid; what do you think the psalmist, King David, meant when he compares fellowship to precipitation from a high, wet place coming down to refresh a low, dry place?

_____

_____

_____

_____

5 Can you describe a time so far when you were able to experience an unmet longing being fulfilled in a healthy way through relationships? For example, maybe there was a time you felt rejected and were accepted by someone after you reached out? Or, perhaps there was a time you felt afraid or anxious and a friend or spouse helped you feel safe after you verbalized your feelings? What was this like, and how did your heart respond to the process? If you have not had this experience, what do you think it could look like in your life? How can this group help?

_____

_____

_____

_____

6 This session video insists "only the parts of us that we allow to be fully known can be fully loved." How does this statement make you feel? Do you agree or disagree? What are some examples of this in your own life?

Read and Reflect

> Let the message of Christ dwell among you richly as you teach and
> admonish one another with all wisdom through psalms, hymns, and
> songs from the Spirit, singing to God with gratitude in your hearts.
> —Colossians 3:16

Read this passage three or four times, either silently as individuals or out loud as a group. What is its message? Consider committing part or all of this passage to memory over the next week.

Respond

This session showed us the value and importance of human relationships in our healing process and encouraged you to make yourself vulnerable and connected in order to grow. What is one big lesson that jumps out in your heart as a matter for prayer and reflection so far, and/or what is one specific action you can commit to try between this session and the next?

Pray

Close your group time by praying in any of the following directions:

1. Thank God for the people in this study and for their willingness to be on the battlefield with you, fighting alongside you for your mind and your God-given identity.

2. Pray for anyone you know who is alone and needs to be enfolded in Christian community. Consider inviting them into your life—they may need to experience community even before they are open to Christ.

3. Pray for anyone in your group having a particularly hard time during this session.

4. Pray that God will give you wisdom about which relationships have the potential to help you thrive, and which are currently unhealthy or likely to cause danger.

DEEPER DIVE

SESSION NINE:
You're Made for More

DON'T JUST "LET GO AND LET GOD"

Read...

Proactive and healing support is not behavior modification. It is a process of inviting God and others to be part of healing the underlying hurts and unresolved areas of our stories that we'd rather avoid—a major objective of the *Resolution Movement* that we launched.* It's easier to blame our old sinful nature than to admit that we may be carrying hurt and unresolved shame that keeps us returning to unhealthy patterns. Proactive and healing support is also not limited to simply talking about sin or unhealthy choices in our lives. It's a *daily* lifestyle of reaching out for help to process the pain and stress in life that often influences the ways we try to cope. We must understand that our sin and unhealthy choices are not random. We sin because we are born sinful, but we also sin because we have been sinned against and have developed ways to cope when that past pain gets triggered. When we are proactive and gain healing support, Jesus matures us into who he created us to be.

When we stop fighting the wrong battles and start implementing proactive and healing support, we can invite Jesus to do his greatest work in the rich soil through

---

* See http://www.resolutionmovement.org.

104

which he has designed healing and growth to take place. He helps us to overcome struggles and our unwanted behaviors. We know this because he's done it with us.

When you encounter an "activating event"—a situation in which you're tempted to turn to an unwanted behavior—take a moment to "press pause" and walk through a process like the following:

1. Identify the negative sensation you're feeling (e.g., is it rejection? feeling unappreciated? etc.).
2. Acknowledge the God-given longing that underlies that sensation (e.g., if you're feeling rejected, you're feeling an unmet longing for acceptance. Or, if you're feeling insecure in some way, the God-given longing that's being threatened or unfulfilled is the longing for the assurance of safety and security).
3. Counter the negative core beliefs you might be telling yourself with the truth (e.g., "I'm feeling worthless and inadequate, but God says I am of great worth in his sight—and people who know me agree with God on that point").
4. Seek the fulfillment of that longing in healthy ways, such as expressing your need to a trusted friend or group of friends (e.g., "I'm feeling devalued because of some things that happened today; I think I could use some reminders that who I am and what I do is appreciated").
5. Repeat the process as often as necessary.

These few steps, repeated quickly and often when you experience an activating event, can reprogram your heart and mind to choose wholeness rather than brokenness. See the diagram on the next page for an illustration of this process.

Assess ...

1 Who is one person you can be vulnerable with to share the areas of your life causing shame?

_____

_____

_____

_____

_____

BROKENNESS VS. WHOLENESS

ACTIVATING EVENT

Any situation that leads to an unmet longing. E.g., rejection from a friend; thinking about an upcoming task or deadline; a spouse or friend being unattentive or angry; feeling misunderstood in a conversation.

UNMET LONGING

The activating event leads to one or more of the Seven Longings going unmet. This often brings with it the pain of the same longings going unmet in past circumstances.

REINFORCE NEGATIVE CORE BELIEFS

Telling yourself lies (e.g., "No one cares," "I am not good enough," "I will never get things right," "I must get revenge," "God isn't good or loving," etc.).

REINFORCE POSITIVE CORE BELIEFS

Telling yourself truth (e.g., "I am not defined by their rejection, opinions, or these feelings; I am loved, worthy, redeemed by Jesus, gifted," etc.).

SEEK FULFILLMENT OF LONGINGS IN UNHEALTHY WAYS

Overworking to feel a sense of worth. Over/Undereating to regain control/feel safe. Looking at porn to feel someone's attention. Procrastination, anxiety, depression, oversleeping, anger, etc.

SEEK FULFILLMENT OF LONGINGS IN HEALTHY WAYS

Reach out to safe people and share your unmet longings and feelings. Ask them to remind you of truth. Experience acceptance and validation. Talk to God and meditate on who he says you are.

FURTHER BROKENNESS

Shame, unresolve, loss of control. Remaining stuck in unwanted behaviors and unhealthy patterns. Repeat the cycle.

FURTHER WHOLENESS

Satisfaction, healing, resilience. Growing into your true identity and overcoming unhealthy patterns. Repeat the cycle.

2 What risks might you face if you continue on in life without being vulnerable and seeking healing?

_____

_____

_____

_____

_____

_____

3 What is the greater vision God might have for your life, to make an impact for him, that is being limited by hurts and unwanted behaviors?

_____

_____

_____

_____

4 What is one step you can take today to get involved in a growth environment?

_____

_____

_____

_____

SESSION TEN

WHAT'S TRUE FOR ME IS TRUE FOR YOU

WELCOME

There is an old party game called "Two Truths and a Lie." In it, you tell two accurate facts about yourself and one total fabrication. You do your best to make them all sound equally believable, speaking sincerely with a straight face, and your listeners try to guess which of the three statements is the lie. You may have played it a few times before. How weird would the game get if the players all had differing philosophies about the nature of truth itself? You would end up with a game named something like "Two Statements Which I Believe to Be Accurate, but with Which You May Adamantly Disagree, Interspersed with One That Is Not Fully Accurate in My Estimation, but Which May Nevertheless Seem Entirely Valid to You." It somehow loses its entertainment value, doesn't it?

Yet this is the level of confusion and hedging with which many people in our cultural moment are now handling the concept of truth. In this study, we have been looking for solid foundations upon which to lay our identities, our self-worth, and our relational ethics. If there is no objective standard, we will struggle greatly. We need to know if there is a reliable standard against which to measure our values, evaluate the quality of our experiences, and relate to one another equitably. In other words, we need to know the truth about Truth, and that's what this session will explore.

SHARE

- Have you ever played "Two Truths and a Lie"? If you have a really good statement for this game that stumps others every time (a false-sounding truth or a true-sounding lie), share it with the group.
- What is your perspective on the nature of absolute truth? How sure are you (give a percentage as your answer) that there are some knowable, consistent things that are equally true for everyone on the face of the earth at all times?

WATCH

Play the video for _Session 10: What's True for Me Is True for You_ from the _Free to Thrive Video Study_. As you watch, use the following outline to record any thoughts, questions, or key points that stand out to you.

- Ernie and Jackie's experience

_____

_____

_____

_____

Culture Shift: 3 Progressions
1. Truth used to be seen as objective: _____.
2. Next, truth was seen as subjective: _____.
3. Now, truth is seen as emotion: _____.

A Universal Truth

- Some things really are subjective, relative, and personal, like ice-cream preferences.

  _____

  _____

  _____

- Moral truth, though, is universal; it is true for all people, in all places, at all times. Most would agree that rape, child abuse, and genocide are wrong, that people are valuable and worth protecting, etc.

  _____

  _____

  _____

- Audrey's experience

  _____

  _____

  _____

The Universal Standard of Truth

- Truth is not a created societal or cultural concept—it is rooted in the nature of God and the person of Jesus Christ.

  _____

  _____

  _____

  _____

- God's nature and character determine moral truth. Truth is not simply something he decides; it is something he is.

  _____

  _____

  _____

  _____

Where the Evidence Points

- More often than not, people's hesitancy to consider the evidence for the Christian faith relates not to their intellectual misgivings, but to the pain and unmet longings in their past. In other words, their concern is not as much about if the Bible is true, as it is about if the One the Bible speaks about is *good* in light of their hurts.

- The only way to know for sure is to investigate the Bible and explore faith firsthand.

DISCUSS

With your group, discuss what you have just watched and explore these concepts in Scripture. Use the following questions to guide your discussion.

1 How much investigating have you done so far into the reliability of Scripture and the possibility of absolute moral truth? Are you convinced about the Bible and Jesus? If not, what might it take to get you there? Share insights and perspectives as a group.

----

2 **Read:** Deuteronomy 32:1–6. What aspects of the Lord's character and nature are described? How do these descriptors make you feel about God? Does this feeling draw you closer, or is it off-putting? Based on these verses, would you say God has the right to set standards for absolute truth?

_____

_____

_____

_____

_____

_____

_____

3 What are some of the things you—or others whom you care about—would list as reasons to question the wisdom and goodness of God? Do you find these arguments compelling? What responses, if any, have you been able to think of when these objections come up?

_____

_____

_____

_____

_____

_____

4 Can you think of any other examples of things in the world that are universal moral truths? Do people ever argue about these, or are they universally accepted?

_____

_____

_____

_____

_____

_____

5 **Read:** James 1:2–18. What jumps out at you when you read this passage? How does God's generosity in giving wisdom encourage you in your investigations of truth? What roles do faith, humility, and perseverance play in our search for truth? What do you think James means when he says that God chose to give us birth through the word of truth? How does truth relate to being God's child?

_____

_____

_____

_____

_____

6 **Read:** Acts 17:24–31. This early sermon, delivered by Paul the apostle in Athens, is very clear about the universality of creation, spiritual hunger, truth, and judgment at the end of the world. It is also clear that all such things have been placed in the hands of Jesus. How might this sermon be heard today if it were preached in the political and cultural center of your nation? How does it speak to you today?

_____

_____

_____

_____

Read and Reflect

> Every good and perfect gift is from above, coming down from the Father
> of the heavenly lights, who does not change like shifting shadows.
>
> —James 1:17

Read this passage three or four times, either silently as individuals or out loud as a group. What is its message? Consider committing part or all of this passage to memory over the next week.

Respond

This session is meant to show you that the security and basis for our growth and satisfaction is rooted in the absolute morality, goodness, and truth embodied by Jesus Christ. Our culture prefers to think of truth as relative, but this leaves us no basis for security and confidence in our identity and no hope of satisfaction in our longings. What is one big lesson that jumps out in your heart as a matter for prayer and reflection so far, and/or what is one specific action you can commit to try between this session and the next?

Pray

Close your group time by praying in any of the following directions:

- Pray and ask God for wisdom in your group's investigation of his truth. If any of your group members are unsure about Jesus and biblical morality, assure them that they are allowed to investigate and are welcome in the group. Ask God to help them feel safe and valued here.
- Pray for clarity and boldness on issues of moral truth, paired with humility and flexibility on all matters of mere personal preference.
- Thank and adore God for his nature—list some things about his character that give you comfort, security, and hope.
- Pray for God's truth to be seen and appreciated by all people, especially as it relates to salvation and the gospel.

DEEPER DIVE

SESSION TEN:
What's True for Me Is True for You

WHO DO YOU SAY THAT I AM?

Read . . .

An overwhelming amount of evidence points to the conclusion that Christianity is true, the Bible is reliable, and God's truth is objective and has bearing on our lives. But despite having all the evidence in the world, we may still find ourselves holding back. We may still refrain from following Jesus. Sometimes our unmet longings run so deep that we blame God and scoff at the thought of surrendering to him. We make assumptions about his character based on the tragedies we have weathered. You may have wondered if Christianity is true, while doubting at a deeper level whether God is good. And how could he be good, when there is much suffering and evil in the world?

When Jesus walked this earth, healing people, teaching, and inviting people into a life of wholeness, he had many skeptics and critics. One day, as he walked with his disciples, the men he had been investing his life in, he asked them what the crowds were saying about him: "Who do people say I am?" They replied, "Some say John the Baptist; others say Elijah; and still others, one of the prophets" (Mark 8:27–28). Then Jesus got to the point:

"But what about *you*?" he asked. "Who do *you* say I am?"

Simon Peter answered, "You are the Messiah, the Son of the living God." (Matthew 16:15–16, italics added)

What about you? Who do *you* say Jesus is? Each of us has an individual decision to make, a conversation to have with Jesus. It's one of surrender or rebellion, friendship or alienation. When we die, we will stand before God, and those who have given their lives to Jesus and know him personally will spend eternity in heaven, a place of wholeness with no more tears, pain, or suffering. Those who don't surrender to Jesus will suffer the consequences of their choice—an eternity apart from God and everything he is, everything good, pleasing, satisfying, and beautiful. But Jesus's invitation, here and now, is for you. Who do you say he is? If you've yet to give your life to Jesus Christ and accept his punishment for your sins through his life, death, and resurrection, we encourage you to do so now, before reading further. Will you weigh the evidence, consider Jesus's love and purpose for you, and make a decision today?

Assess ...

1 Before you explored truth in this session, did you think it was significant? If so, why? After working through this session, what have you learned about truth?

_____

_____

_____

_____

_____

2 In what ways has our culture's shift toward subjective and emotional truth affected your view of truth?

_____

_____

_____

_____

_____

3 What bearings do the truths explored in this session have on your identity, value, and purpose in life?

_____

_____

_____

_____

_____

4 If you wish to learn more, will you consider obtaining and reading Josh's books, in particular *Evidence That Demands a Verdict* and *More Than a Carpenter*?

_____

_____

_____

_____

YOUR MOVE

WELCOME

Well, this study is nearing an end, but your journey to satisfaction in your deep longings and freedom from unwanted behaviors is still just beginning. You have been given many concepts to think about and many tools to use, but it all comes down to a simple question: what will your next move be? Will you dig deep, engage some growing environments, and risk regular vulnerability? Or will you consider for a time before moving ahead? Maybe you are planning to just back off and save all this for another day?

Regardless, this session is intended to help your group wrap up, map out some next steps you can take as individuals or together, and commit to the process of long-term healing. What you do with everything is up to you, but we sincerely hope you will do the hard work, use the resources provided in this study guide, and continue to trust and walk with these friends. Let's dig in one more time and think about your next move . . .

SHARE

- What is something about this process you didn't expect, but which has been good and rewarding? How have your group members blessed and challenged you up to this point? What are some things you will take with you?

- Have you ever put off something significant you needed or wanted to do? It could've been a project on your home, going to the doctor, a schoolwork assignment, etc. How did you feel when you finally got working on it?

WATCH

Play the video for *Session 11: Your Move* from the *Free to Thrive Video Study*. As you watch, use the following outline to record any thoughts, questions, or key points that stand out to you.

Motivation for Moving Forward

- More of Josh's story

_____

_____

_____

_____

_____

- Ernie and Jackie's experience

_____

_____

_____

_____

_____

The Consequences of Chaos

- Our primary motivation to change comes down to one of two things: either pain or pleasure.

_____

_____

_____

_____

- We have choices we can make, but we can't decide the consequences of these choices—those are set by God.

_____

_____

_____

The Stakes Are High

- The consequences of staying stuck in unwanted behaviors are devastating.

_____

_____

_____

A Greater Vision

- The rewards of change and greater satisfaction give us joy and bring meaning out of suffering.

_____

_____

_____

- Fedel's experience (Anthony Flagg)

_____

_____

_____

- More of Ben's story

_____

_____

_____

- Meaning and growth through tragedy

_____

_____

_____

- This is the thriving life Jesus promised to give his disciples—one of meaning, satisfaction, real change, and freedom! It isn't easy, but it is *worth it*!

  _____
  _____
  _____
  _____
  _____

- Audrey's experience

  _____
  _____
  _____
  _____
  _____

- Monica's experience

  _____
  _____
  _____
  _____
  _____

Your Next Move

- There are resources and next steps outlined in the back of this study guide, at resolutionmovement.org, and in the book *Free to Thrive*—please consider using these, as well as the relationships you have built in this group, to move ahead and engage ongoing healing.

  _____
  _____
  _____
  _____
  _____

DISCUSS

With your group, discuss what you have just watched and explore these concepts in Scripture. Use the following questions to guide your discussion.

1 If you simply did the basics you have learned in this study, what would that look like? How much time per day or week would it take? What if you really dug in and took it to the next level? What would that look like, and what would it cost in terms of time and treasure?

_____

_____

_____

_____

2 **Read:** Proverbs 4:20–27. What do these verses seem to say about learning, investing in emotional and spiritual health, and growth? How does this relate to the next move you might make? What might it be worth?

_____

_____

_____

_____

3 What are some of the things discussed in this study that hit a nerve and need further investigation? What do the members of your group have to offer in terms of advice or encouragement about who could help, what to dig into next, and how to pray?

_____

_____

_____

_____

4 **Read:** 1 Corinthians 9:24–27. What inspiration can you draw from these examples of training which the apostle Paul uses? Have you ever been guilty of running aimlessly or beating the air in your efforts to find satisfaction and freedom? Will this time be different? Why or why not?

_____

_____

_____

_____

5 What would it look like if you made your growth and progress matters of strict training by the power of the Holy Spirit? How might you engage in further learning? What counselors, books, advisors, friends, and mentors would you want to call next? What other activities, loyalties, and distractions are currently competing with such an investment?

_____

_____

_____

_____

6 **Read:** Philippians 3:12–16. Describe the prize you are shooting for in your walk with Jesus and your growth journey. What would it mean to go all in? What does it mean to "live up to what we have already attained"? How will you go about doing that? How can the members of your group help you as individuals? As a whole group? What might you do together to keep this support going, and what next steps can you take for building up each other?

_____

_____

_____

_____

Read and Reflect

> And let us run with perseverance the race marked out for us, fixing our eyes on Jesus, the pioneer and perfecter of faith. For the joy set before him he endured the cross, scorning its shame, and sat down at the right hand of the throne of God.
>
> —Hebrews 12:1b–2

Read this passage three or four times, either silently as individuals or out loud as a group. What is its message? Consider committing part or all of this passage to memory over the next week.

Respond

This session pointed out that the next steps in this process are in your hands—God is ready to meet you in your journey, but you need to commit to your next move. What is one big lesson that jumps out in your heart as a matter for prayer and reflection so far, and/or what is one specific action you can commit to try?

Pray

Close your group time by praying in any of the following directions:

- Pray for everyone in your group, one person at a time—be sure to ask the Lord for wisdom and insight about the best way each one can move ahead next.
- Thank God for the unique contributions and investment each person in the group has made.
- Pray for Josh McDowell and Ben Bennett and their ministries. Invite God to bless them, this curriculum, and all who study in groups like yours.
- Pray for those who don't yet know the joy and comfort of salvation in Jesus. Ask God to lead you to share until everyone in your sphere of influence has had a chance to hear the good news of freedom and a thriving life in Jesus.

SESSION ELEVEN:
Your Move

A GREATER VISION

Read...

God designed human beings to be motivated to grow and heal by seeing beyond the pain of change and focusing on the reward. He designed us to be motivated by a greater vision, greater meaning, and greater purpose. He intends for us to live a life of thriving, in light of a greater reward, as we find meaning in our pain. God wants us to know the joy set before *us*. He wants to set us free from our unwanted behaviors. He wants to heal our pain. He wants to use us in the lives of others to help bring healing and freedom. He wants us to experience greater connection with himself and others. He wants us to know our true value and worth. He wants us to boldly share with others his message of healing, forgiveness, and joy that is found in a personal relationship with him, a relationship that is available to all.

Jesus promised that when we surrender to him what we're holding onto, we will find true life (Matthew 16:25). When we lay down these things—unwanted behaviors, unforgiveness, negative core beliefs about God, self, and others—and take strides to follow him in all areas, we will find purpose, thriving, and maximum satisfaction.

Consider what it would look like to live from a place of positive core beliefs and your longings being met in healthy ways by God, yourself, and others, rather than living in the chaos of lies and unwanted behaviors. Think through what rewards and positive benefits you might experience on the other side of your healing journey. The following chart will help you consider some of the ways this could take place.

Longing	Results of My Longings Being Met
Acceptance	Secure in my value and how much I'm loved. Not compromising my standards, schedule, or capacity in an attempt to get people's acceptance or approval. Not reacting to lies and coping through unwanted behaviors. Being able to rest in my acceptance rather than being exhausted by striving to feel accepted.
Appreciation	Knowing that God approves of my effort and is proud of me no matter what. Being secure in knowing that what I do is meaningful and matters in this world, rather than being unsure and always wondering if my life means anything.
Affection	Respecting myself and others rather than seeking out affection through unhealthy people or inappropriate interactions.
Access	Knowing that I am worth people's time and love, and that I'm not a burden. Believing God is always close, interested in the finite details of my life, and willing to engage with me.
Attention	Being confident in my thoughts, opinions, and choices. Knowing how to get to know others, take interest in their lives, and celebrate the differences.
Affirmation of Feelings	Knowing that my thoughts and feelings are legitimate and part of what it means to be human. Knowing that I am understood, seen, and not alone.
Assurance of Safety	Free from anxiety, obsessive thoughts, and knowing that God cares for my every need and will protect me.

Assess . . .

1 How liberating would it be to live in a thriving way?

_____

_____

_____

2 How much of your mental space and time might be freed up as you find healing from lies and unwanted behaviors?

_____

_____

_____

3 What would it look like for you to have your longings met and be free from your unwanted behaviors?

_____

_____

_____

4 How might your connection with God and others increase?

_____

_____

_____

5 How might you experience a greater capacity to love and give to others?

_____

_____

_____

CLOSING THOUGHTS

Throughout this study, you've explored the Wholeness Apologetic model. Wholeness and healing happen as you continue to live into the concepts we have explored. See "God's Design for Healing" in the diagram on page 22 for a summary of how we heal and move forward in wholeness. We've also shared about the *Resolution Movement* and how those part of it are overcoming unmet longings and unwanted behaviors.

We want to invite you into the *Resolution Movement* as well. Join with us. Recommend this study to your pastor, youth pastor, or a friend you know. Check out our website (www.resolutionmovement.org) and pages on social media for more posts, videos, and resources. Continue getting equipped to overcome unmet longings and unwanted behaviors.

In the *Deeper Dive* exercises between sessions, you've found a variety of tools for further study and growth. These exercises will help you take more steps to apply the principles of this study into your life. We know that information without application is of little help in the growth process, so we encourage you to go back and use these tools if you haven't yet. Go through them and share the results with a safe and trusted person in your life.

Finally, we've compiled further recommended books and resources that deal with specific issues we have addressed in this study. Check out the list of recommended resources on the following pages to continue to grow in overcoming unwanted behaviors and experiencing the fulfillment of your unmet longings.

We encourage you to continue this journey in experiencing healing and freedom and living into wholeness. Make a practice of identifying and seeking the fulfillment of your unmet longings. Get help and support for your unwanted behaviors. Take this process one step at a time, one longing at a time, and one day at a time. Jesus has set before you a thriving life into which he is inviting you.

LEADING
THIS GROUP

GROUP SIZE

The *Free to Thrive Video Study* and the *Free to Thrive Study Guide* are designed to be experienced in a group setting such as a Bible study, church staff training, Sunday school class, or any small group gathering. To ensure everyone has enough time to participate in discussions, we recommend that large groups break up into smaller groups of four to six people each. The matters discussed can be weighty at times, and smaller group sizes facilitate courageous sharing and ample time for mutual disclosure.

MATERIALS NEEDED

Each participant should have his or her own study guide, which includes notes for video segments, directions for activities, and discussion questions, as well as suggested personal application and a Deeper Dive section to deepen learning between sessions.

TIMING

Each session will take between ninety minutes and two hours. For those who have less time available to meet, you can use fewer questions for discussion.

FACILITATION

Each group should appoint a facilitator who is responsible for starting the video and keeping track of time during discussions and activities. Facilitators may also read questions aloud and monitor discussions, prompting participants to respond and ensuring that everyone has the opportunity to participate. The facilitator should also guide the group members through the prayer prompts and encourage them to dig into the Deeper Dive sections.

PERSONAL STUDIES

Maximize the impact of this curriculum with additional study between group sessions. Suggestions for further study and reflection are provided following each session. Feel free to engage with these optional study materials as much or as little as you need.

TOOLS FOR GROWTH

THE MET AND UNMET LONGINGS TABLE

Use this table to identify the extent to which your longings went unmet in your life growing up. Doing so will help you understand why you might struggle to this day with specific unmet longings and help you to begin to find healing. For each category, respond with one of the following: Hardly Met, Sometimes Met, Mostly Met.

Longings	Mom	Dad	Siblings	Friends
1. Acceptance to be included, loved, and approved of as you are, no matter what.				
2. Appreciation to be thanked or encouraged for what you have done.				

Longings	Mom	Dad	Siblings	Friends
3. Affection to be cared for with gentle touch or emotional engagement.				
4. Access to have the consistent emotional and physical presence of key figures.				
5. Attention to be known and understood with someone entering your world.				
6. Affirmation of Feelings to have our feelings affirmed, validated, or confirmed by others.				
7. Assurance of Safety to feel safe, protected, and provided for emotionally, physically, and financially.				

After filling out the table, identify which three longings went unmet the most growing up:

1.

2.

3.

What negative core beliefs might you have about yourself from these unmet longings?

1.

2.

3.

What negative core beliefs might you have about God from these unmet longings?

1.

2.

3.

What negative core beliefs might you have about others from these unmet longings?

1.

2.

3.

See "Renewing the Mind" on the following pages for ways to overcome these negative core beliefs.

RENEWING THE MIND

Do not conform to the pattern of this world, but be transformed by the renewing of your mind. *(Romans 12:2)*

We demolish arguments and every pretension that sets itself up against the knowledge of God, and we take captive every thought to make it obedient to Christ. *(2 Corinthians 10:5)*

Use the following exercise as one way to begin rewiring your brain daily. When unmet longings and lies come up, meditate on these truths and experiences. We encourage you to utilize this practice to rewire negative core beliefs about God and others as well.

STEP ONE

Identify three core lies you believe about yourself, God, and others (e.g., *I'm worthless, I'm unlovable, I can never measure up, I can't trust people, if I let people get close they will hurt me, God doesn't love me*). Often, these are directly tied to some of the painful experiences in your life growing up.

1.

2.

3.

STEP TWO

Identify a verse of Scripture to challenge each lie (e.g., *I'm not worthless because I'm loved, as 1 John 3:1 [ESV] says—"See what kind of love the Father has given to us, that we should be called children of God; and so we are"*).

1.

2.

3.

STEP THREE

Identify a time in life when you experienced the truth of this Scripture and when God communicated this to you (e.g., *My first year in college, I recommitted my life to Christ at a worship gathering. During that experience I felt so loved and accepted by God and others and experienced what it meant to be a loved child of God, as 1 John 3:1 says*).

Visualizing this past experience engages the limbic system, the emotional brain, the same place our experiences of unmet longings are recorded. This helps the truth of Scripture sink into our heart and renew our mind.

1.

2.

3.

PROACTIVE SUPPORT

We encourage you to identify one or two people you can begin talking with throughout each week about how you're truly doing. You may want to go through this study with them, but at minimum we encourage you to use the following questions to support one another in the growth process.

1. Which of the Seven Longings are going unmet in my life this week?
2. What am I feeling and believing as a result?
3. What unwanted behaviors might I desire to go to in order to cope with these unmet longings?
4. How can I seek their fulfillment through God and others?

ADDITIONAL RESOURCES

In this section you'll find great additional resources for various issues related to unmet longings and unwanted behaviors. From counseling organizations to support for your spiritual life, these resources offer great next steps to this study, helping you experience further healing and growth (for more resources, check out resolutionmovement.org /resources).

COMPULSIVE UNWANTED BEHAVIORS

Four Streams Coaching (fourstreamscoaching.com)

An organization offering online coaching, articles, and support for mental health and behavioral health issues. Its online platform offers daily support, empowering a movement of connection, freedom, and integrity by equipping and inspiring its users.

Genesis Process (genesisprocess.org)

The Genesis Process provides a biblical and neurochemical understanding of what is broken and causes our self-destruction. Through videos, books, small group resources, and events, this organization offers a groundbreaking approach to understand and overcome unwanted behaviors.

How People Grow (cloudtownsend.com)

Authors Dr. Henry Cloud and Dr. John Townsend unlock age-old keys to growth from Scripture to help people resolve issues of relationships, maturity, emotional problems, and overall spiritual growth. In this theological foundation to their best-selling book *Boundaries*, they discuss key concepts to help individuals understand and overcome unwanted behaviors.

IITAP (iitap.com)

The International Institute for Trauma and Addiction Professionals (IITAP) is a global leader among practitioners who treat addictive and compulsive behaviors. IITAP provides a wealth of articles and resources, as well as a therapist locator to find the best support in your area.

SEXUAL ISSUES

Pure Desire Ministries (puredesire.org)

Your safe place to find hope and healing. A biblically and clinically sound organization offering counseling, small group resources, blogs, podcasts, and books to help individuals understand and overcome the effects of unwanted sexual behavior. Its groundbreaking book, *Pure Desire*, by Dr. Ted Roberts, is a must-read and a great starting point.

Faithful & True (faithfulandtrue.com)

A Christian counseling ministry specializing in the treatment of unwanted sexual behavior, support for struggling spouses, and guidance for couples who have experienced relational betrayal. It offers counseling, weekend intensives, small group resources, blogs, podcasts, and books.

The Freedom Fight (thefreedomfight.org)

A Christian-based and neuroscience-informed online recovery program for unwanted sexual behavior. This resource offers an anonymous and tech-based approach to experiencing freedom.

God Loves Sex (theallendercenter.org)

This book by Drs. Dan Allender and Tremper Longman III offers a truly liberating, godly view of holy sensuality. Pairing psychological insight with sound biblical scholarship, it brings desire and sex out into the open, allowing Christians of any age and marital status to understand sex the way God meant it to be.

Unwanted (jay-stringer.com)

In this book, therapist Jay Stringer explores the "why" behind self-destructive sexual choices. Through his groundbreaking research, Stringer found that unwanted sexual behavior can be both shaped by and predicted based on the parts of our story—past and present—that remain unaddressed. When we pay attention to our unwanted sexual desires and identify the unique reasons that trigger them, the path of healing is revealed.

ABUSE AND TRAUMA

Allender Center (theallendercenter.org)

One of the leading Christian organizations specializing in support for abuse and trauma. This theologically rich and psychologically deep organization offers trainings, specialized counseling, blogs, podcasts, and books to help individuals find healing from abuse and trauma.

EMDR (emdr.com)

EMDR (Eye Movement Desensitization and Reprocessing) is psychotherapy that enables people to heal from the symptoms and emotional distress that are the result of disturbing life experiences. Repeated studies show that by using EMDR therapy, people can experience the benefits of psychotherapy that once took years to make a difference. It is widely assumed that severe emotional pain requires a long time to heal. EMDR therapy shows that the mind can in fact heal from psychological trauma just as much as the body recovers from physical trauma. Check out the website to locate an EMDR specialist in your area.

Healing the Wounded Heart (theallendercenter.org)

This book by Dan B. Allender addresses issues of sexual abuse across social, religious, and gender lines. He provides a biblically based path for survivors to find healing and restoration through God's help, love, and mercy.

Please Tell! A Child's Story about Sexual Abuse (amazon.com)

Written and illustrated by a young girl who was sexually molested by a family member, this book reaches out to other children in a way that no adult can. Jessie's words carry the message, "It's o.k. to tell; help can come when you tell." This book is an excellent tool for therapists, counselors, child protection workers, teachers, and parents dealing with children affected by sexual abuse.

MENTAL HEALTH

Four Streams Coaching (fourstreamscoaching.com)

An organization offering online coaching, articles, and support for mental health and behavioral health issues. Its online platform offers daily support, empowering a movement of connection, freedom, and integrity by equipping and inspiring its users.

AACC (aacc.net)

The American Association of Christian Counselors offers articles, courses, and a large network of coaches and therapists in your area.

To Write Love on Her Arms (twloha.com)

A movement dedicated to presenting hope and finding help for people struggling with depression, addiction, self-injury, and suicide. TWLOHA exists to encourage, inform, inspire, and invest directly into treatment and recovery.

Better Help (betterhelp.com)

An organization offering online professional counseling in an accessible, affordable, convenient, and private way. Through its online platform, anyone who struggles with life's challenges can get help anytime, anywhere.

THE BRAIN

The Brain That Changes Itself (normandoidge.com)

In this revolutionary look at the brain, psychiatrist and psychoanalyst Norman Doidge, M.D., provides an introduction to both the brilliant scientists championing neuroplasticity and the people whose lives they've transformed. From stroke patients learning to speak again to the remarkable case of a woman born with half a brain that rewired itself to work as a whole, *The Brain That Changes Itself* will permanently alter the way we look at our brains, human nature, and human potential.

Switch On Your Brain (drleaf.com)

This book by Dr. Caroline Leaf offers breakthrough neuroscientific research. What you are thinking every moment of every day becomes a physical reality in your brain and body, which affects your optimal mental and physical health. Based solidly on the latest neuroscientific research on the brain, as well as Dr. Caroline Leaf's clinical experience and research, you will learn how thoughts impact our spirit, soul, and body.

Wired for Intimacy (ivpress.com)

In this book, neuroscientist and researcher William Struthers explains how pornography affects the male brain and what we can do about it. Because we are embodied beings, viewing pornography changes how the brain works, how we form memories, and how we make attachments. By better understanding the biological realities of our sexual development, we can cultivate healthier sexual perspectives and interpersonal relationships.

SPIRITUAL

Cru (cru.org)

Cru, the largest missionary organization in the world, consists of various ministries for teens, college students, young professionals, and married couples in your area. Check out its online videos, articles, and ministries to take the next step in your spiritual journey.

The Cure (trueface.org)

This book offers a unique and biblical understanding of the character of God. Many of us couldn't measure up to a standard we created, so we convinced ourselves it was God's. We read his words through our grid of shame and felt ourselves fall farther and farther behind. We took it out on each other: judging, comparing, faking, splintering. We all need to understand who God truly is, for it impacts the way we live, love, and see ourselves and other people.

Church.org

Find a church in your area and get connected to invest in your spiritual growth and serve others.

The Unshakable Truth (josh.org)

This book uniquely presents apologetics relationally, focusing on how Christianity's doctrines affect relationships. The authors ground every concept in the overarching story of creation, incarnation, and re-creation. They cover core concepts of the Christian faith and how we can know it is true. Topics include who God truly is, self-image and human value, evidence for the deity of Christ, evidence for the reliability of Scripture, and how we grow.

See Yourself as God Sees You (josh.org)

This book uses stories and Scripture to establish and remind you of what God says about who you are, so that you can discover and live according to your true identity.

10 Ways to Say "I Love You": Embracing a Love That Lasts (josh.org)

A book to help married couples learn to express and fulfill the Seven Longings in ways that will deepen and broaden a lifelong love.

How to Be a Hero to Your Kids (josh.org)

This book will position parents to meet their kids' longings in healthy and lasting ways.

Serving others until the whole world hears about Jesus.

Josh McDowell
A CRU MINISTRY